VINEYARD
SUPERNATURAL

VINEYARD
SUPERNATURAL

True Ghost Stories
From America's
Most Haunted Island

HOLLY MASCOTT NADLER

Photographs by NANCY WHITE

Down East

IN MEMORIAM

To my Great Grandma Olga of Lowell, Massachusetts
My father, Larry Mascott
And my departed island friends,
extraordinary people all:
Ed Coogan, Nan Reault, Phil Craig, Tami Pine,
Steve Ellis, John Morelli, and Dawn Greeley

Let's keep in touch!

ISBN (13-digit): 978-0-89272-755-1
Library of Congress Cataloging-in-Publication Data
available upon request.
Cover Design by Miroslaw Jurek
Interior Design by Lynda Chilton
Cover photograph © Alison Shaw/Solus Photography/Veer
Printed at Versa Press

5   4   3   2   1

BOOKS·MAGAZINE·ONLINE
www.downeast.com
Distributed to the trade by
National Book Network

CONTENTS

AUTHOR'S NOTE

I know this from having written two collections of true ghost stories: Even though Americans are more open than ever to the possibilities of a spirit world, other dimensions, and things that go bump in the night besides broken refrigerator belts, it's still darn hard for people relating their tales to allow the writer to use their real names. One of these fine days we'll all be able to tell our personal accounts of the paranormal without feeling that at the same time we're being fitted for straitjackets.

Here's how I've dealt in the following pages with varying levels of skittishness in this regard. For people who've been willing to let me use their full names, I've used full names. For those who said, "Please keep my identity anonymous," I've stated that their identities have been kept anonymous. For those who hemmed and hawed, I've used only their first names. In a few cases, when I've decided it would be awkward to call people, say, Girl Number One and Girl Number Two, I've given them fictitious first names followed by asterisks.

Finally, over the years I've filed away in my noggin stories from people I'm met at parties or street corners or fundraisers for local politicians. These folks are described as I've summoned them up from my memory. Who knows what their names were; it was only a little more than a year go that Down East Books and I decided the time was right to produce a second Vineyard ghost book, and only since then have I whipped out a pen and a fifty-nine-cent notebook and said, "Tell me everything!"

I will say this about the details of the upcoming tales: I often have trouble remembering what I had for lunch, but I never forget a good ghost story, whether the experiences were my own or related to me twenty years ago.

WHY WE'RE SO HAUNTED

It's finally happening. In the oldest parts of our country—of which Martha's Vineyard is one—we've stacked up layer upon layer of human history, with all the dramas, clashes, and lost souls imprinted on the air like a *tiramisu* of sugar, cake, and mascarpone cheese all squashed in a glass bowl.

This island is so richly haunted because it has drawn to its shores many of America's most restless seekers without providing them with any lasting comfort or solace, beginning with the original band of Puritans who tried to Christianize the resident Indians but ended up killing most of them with European diseases. In the nineteenth century we had a continuous clash between the sacred and the profane as religious groups looked for God and the tourists arriving on their heels looked for saloons and cathouses and cheap real estate. For those with means, the island holds an irresistible beauty, but this ragged, soil-poor land has forced many of the less fortunate inhabitants away to perish at sea (or, in contemporary terms, to be cast adrift in a larger world of asphalt landscapes and death in living).

This is also a place where for centuries secrets have been kept—aided and abetted by reporters and historians—in a manner that jeopardizes the mental health of the living and the psychical health of the dead. When this happens, negative vortices flourish. In these places angels fear to tread, and so do your run-of-the-mill visiting spirits. With the telling of these stories, we can only hope that some of those blockages in our landscape might at last become unstuck.

Good, bad, and indifferent, we've got hosts of ghosts. The Vineyard is now on a par with ghost-riddled England, though in both New and Olde England the spirit world has put its own regional stamp on ghostly legends. Instead of chain-clanking dungeons, Martha's Vineyard has spectral schooners, and instead of castles with ghostly knights and ladies, we entertain the wraiths of Native Americans, runaway slaves, pirates, and mariners, many of them touching down in old captains' houses or doll-sized Victorian cottages, or hovering in the vicinity of eighteenth-century tombstones that lie forgotten alongside twisting dirt roads.

———

Vineyarders have always lived just far enough out to sea that in our long lonely winters we may turn a bit mad, hemmed in by frozen shores instead of asylum walls. On the other hand, unlike Nantucket and other more remote islands, Martha's Vineyard is close enough—seven miles—to the mainland that the tidal currents of the real world keep things stirred up here.

There's another element in our psychical makeup that I feel compelled to mention: Those of us who live here year-round without trust funds or fortunes made elsewhere are often deeply apprehensive because it's so very hard to earn a living on this rock where there are never enough jobs. It has always been this way: the summer's three months of income barely stretching through the desolate months of winter.

And yet we're loath to leave. The rest of the world seems unnecessarily harsh, unnecessarily . . . ugly. Here, during an early morning walk you can watch a formation of geese flapping skyward, observe pink mists rising over a saltwater inlet, and pass by a twinkling, frosted field stretching to a stand of snow-capped pine trees. Living here feels like a doomed love affair; it brings you no peace, but you know your lover is more beautiful, more exciting, and infinitely more kind than anyone else in the world. This brand of agony and ecstasy attracts both angels and demons to the Vineyard. It also recalls certain souls who have ostensibly passed on but who find it just as difficult to leave the island in death as in life. Call it a spirit world agoraphobia.

—

A gentleman from Dublin who visited my bookstore recently said with a small amount of pride, "In Ireland, ghosts're thick as molasses."

Here too.

Lately I've been advising people to stop ignoring the eerie stimuli bombarding their sixth sense, and to take note of the experiences that let us know we're not alone here, we easily frightened, fragile, alive ones. A normal person's day is packed with the supernatural, and yet we unceasingly convince ourselves we only imagined the evidence of it; what just happened *couldn't* have happened.

Even those of us who believe we dwell within a prism of universes are habitually blind, deaf, and dumb to most of it: the footsteps in the attic (as we remind ourselves we have no attic, hence no footsteps), the stunning coincidences, the precognition of a phone call or a visit, the lost object that suddenly seems to find *us*, the tap on the shoulder when no one's there, the charged atmosphere that repels us as we round the corner of a two-hundred-year-old shipping station, an old farmhouse that gives us the willies—the same one where the owners have moved out, where painters and carpenters have refused to work alone in certain rooms, and where a neighbor has heard screams erupting late at night from the "empty" third floor.

My own haunted life on the Vineyard has its cycles and seasons. Sometimes months go by when nothing happens, but then there are the active periods . . . . Here's an account of a typical day during one of those times.

I live over my little bookstore in Oak Bluffs, and I start each morning by leading my Boston terrier, Huxley, through the shop as we head out for our early morning walk. A little plump, square book with a green cover sits on the counter: *Everyday Positive Thinking* by Louise L. Hay & Friends. Hmm . . . I know I catalogued this into the system the previous afternoon, finding a spot for it on my Mind/Spirit shelves. I remember it vividly because a volume of such dinky proportions is hard to place with the normal-sized books.

Another oddity: The door to the basement, closed and locked the night before, stands open—again. One of the tiny decorative lamps under the high ceiling is dark, but I don't bother to drag over the stepladder; the light will fuse on again by itself. (I learned this lesson after months of changing perfectly good, working bulbs.)

It's a sparkling blue and gold October morning, and

Huxley and I head through the Campground, a village of three hundred exquisitely preserved Queen Anne cottages. Most of the owners have left for the season. Pastel shutters are closed and tightly fastened. The gingerbread-style porches have been cleared of their wicker furniture. I hear the lonely tinkling of a set of overlooked wind-chimes. I can feel the brooding regard of nineteenth-century grandmothers, restored to younger versions of themselves—and restored, now and then, to this place. But this impression of mine is personal, subjectively perceptual, and even though I've glimpsed two ghosts here—one a Confederate soldier, the other a more modern figure in a silvery grey tee-shirt—I rarely volunteer this information unless I'm certain of an open-minded reception. We so-called sensitives (I think of it more accurately as susceptibles) have learned how to at least *appear* sane.

Later I tell my friend, petite, brunette art dealer Paula, about my pipe dream of selling the bookstore and spending at least six months each year in a monastery in Italy. "I feel Assisi calling to me," I say.

She glances over my shoulder and exclaims, "Wow! Two monks were just staring in your window!"

Monks? In true monkish robes? In America? Nowadays Catholic clergy wear sneakers and Red Sox tee-shirts, do they not? I pad outside to see for myself. Sure enough, heading up the street are two friars clad in plain brown cassocks with hoods, a monastic *couture* made famous by the thirteenth-century saint, Francis of Assisi.

In the evening of this typical day when the force is with me, Huxley and I stroll down to the harbor. Only a couple of sleek sailboats rest at anchor this late in the year; the other vessels are all hard-working fishermen's trawlers. As Hux and I wander along the seawall, then head home through the meandering lanes of the Campground, at least one of the tall town lamps winks off as we pass underneath. When this first started happening, a couple of weeks before, I'd paid little attention.

Then I realized that this nightly plunge into darkness had been occurring way too often, with me and my dog always perfectly centered beneath the halogen globe as it went dark. The problem has to be more than a mechanical glitch. This was a poltergeist greeting of *"We're here, babe!"* on this haunted isle.

———

A serious theme is growing within the carnival atmosphere of ghost magazines, paranormal societies, and Web sites where people share their photographs of mysterious glowing orbs of disembodied energy. Fifteen or twenty years ago, few Americans had ever heard of guided walking tours past haunted houses, but now we find these walks everywhere, from Key West all the way up through the Civil War battle sites, Savannah, Charlestown, Cape Cod and the Islands, Boston, and most dramatically, Salem, Massachusetts, whose last Halloween Week attracted so many visitors that traffic came to a standstill on Interstate 95 a few miles to the west.

Ghost stories have always been fun. Let's not disparage or cease to enjoy their entertainment value. But writers and researchers into the paranormal such as Paul F. Eno (*God, Ghosts, and Human Destiny*), the Vineyard's own Reverend S. Ralph Harlow (*Life After Death*), and, more than a hundred years ago, the brilliant psychologist and philosopher and cofounder of the American Society for Psychical Research, William James (*Varieties of Religious Experience*) have found within the nether world of spirits a vital tool for their own personal theology.

And how could it *not* become personal? A strict adherence to a single faith is almost unheard of today in the ranks of the educated, introspective, seeking segment of the population. Rarely do you meet an agnostic raised as an Episcopalian who hasn't delved into Buddhist meditation, a reform rabbi who isn't conversant about Julian of Norwich or Jalaluddin Rumi, or anyone at a fundraiser who hasn't attended at least one Hindu *darshan*, or had a tarot reading, a reiki treatment, or a good soak in a Lakota sweat lodge. Recently I saw a bumper sticker that proclaimed: *GOD IS TOO BIG TO BE STUFFED INTO A SINGLE RELIGION.* (*Caveat emptor*: Anyone who doesn't agree with this philosophy probably shouldn't be reading this book.)

And how does a credible ghost story or direct experience of the supernatural play into some sort of connection with the Divine? Well, first, in our search for a vital Reality, we long to know that there's more to life than what our five senses reveal to us. When a deceased relative causes her favorite rose bush to bloom in January, or a transparent woman in a Victorian nightgown appears at the end of our bed, we become aware that other dimensions exist, that if there's a world beyond death, there may also be multiple universes snapping, crackling, and popping within us and without us—and all of it connected, right down to the smallest particle of the atom as well as to the farthest electron spinning at the outer rim of time and space.

If you start with a ghost and end up pondering quantum psychics, you realize it all comes together with a big red bow and a gift card signed *God* or *Spirit* or *Ground of All Being* or (fill in your own blank).

Scratch the surface of anyone fascinated by ghosts and you'll find a natural-born theologian.

HOW WE COLLABORATE WITH GHOSTS

Theology aside, we must not lose sight of the entertainment value of a good story of the supernatural.

Who's having a better time around a campfire when a tale is being told about Bigfoot? Is it the listener who shudders and steals a glance into the pitch black woods, then, stifling a giggle, grabs the arm of her companion? Or is it the guy seated on the far side of the orange embers who rolls his eyes and sneers, "You suckers are falling for this?!" Not only is this uncharming cynic having no fun, but everyone around him is having less fun because he's there.

I learned this lesson—about the pure glee that accompanies an open mind—on a seventh-grade debating team when the hot-button topic was whether UFOs really exist. I volunteered for the *No* side, thinking this would be a shoo-in to win the debate, since all smart people are science oriented, and science has never (supposedly) come up with a single shred of evidence for UFOs.

Boy, was I wrong. About the shoo-in part.

As we members of the smart, scientific *No* team rattled off data about how prohibitively long it would take for intelligent life from another galaxy to shuttle here, and why would extraterrestrials be interested in our little planet anyway, tucked as it is in the Podunk of the Milky Way, the other side of the debate—the *Yes* kids—rolled out one juicy UFO saga after the next.

Suddenly I wished with all my heart I'd volunteered for the *Yes* team. I would have *loved* to be the one relating an eyewitness account of a farmer outside Wichita who, one evening while driving his tractor, was suddenly blinded by a flurry of incoming lights, after which his three-ton vehicle, with him still in the driver's seat, *levitated* fifty feet off the ground, hovered over his grain silo, spun right, then left, then *exploded in a red fireball*, after which, two hours later, the farmer woke up in the middle of his own frozen asparagus field. He was able to prove this whole episode truly happened by holding up his hand with the tractor's steering wheel—all that remained of the beleaguered vehicle—*heat-soldered* to his palm.

Ludicrous? Of course! I would only believe this story if I had been seated beside the farmer on the tractor-turned-helicopter. But it *could* have happened, right? That half-second pause to consider the possibility, however slim, lends an extra delight to the tale—to all tales. (In fact, we're disappointed when the supernatural element is removed. Consider John Travolta's paranormally induced hyper-genius in the movie *Phenomenon* turning out to be a simple brain tumor; didn't that take all the starch out of the story?)

So, by all means, let us exercise good judgment, but at the same time let us leave ourselves open to the possibility that something truly weird and wonderful could happen to any one of us. Being smart and open-minded and possessed of a sense of humor will enable us to change the world.

———

Finally, we alive ones work in collaboration with all the dead souls, angelic forces, and negative entities with whom we share a common space. This movie we're filming together has a longer credit roll than any mere Hollywood production.

Here's a sample scenario, assembled from several true stories:

A brand-new six-thousand-square-foot trophy house sits on a cliff overlooking the Atlantic Ocean on the southwesternmost part of the island. Five hundred years ago, a tribe of Pokonockets pitched their tents here in the summer. They fished from the beach below and gathered wild grapes, beach plums, and bayberries in the surrounding fields. As the years went by, the tribe slowly moved its tents farther west and the original site became their burial ground.

In the mid-1600s when the first European settlers started making tracks on the island, a single white male with a high threshold for privacy bought this acreage and built a rustic homestead only a notch above the meanest shack. He married a young Pokonocket woman with whom he sired a family of thirteen children, nine of whom survived into adulthood. The man and his family were absorbed into the native community.

As time moved on, the homestead grew to include a bigger house, a barn, a tool shed, and other outbuildings. Later, additional farmsteads were built for the grown children and their families. Because the Native Americans had been interred without markers, no one paid any attention to whether the structures were placed over human remains.

But the spirit world remembers.

A bit of each departed soul seems to remain with the small plot of ground where its memory was once observed by the living. Even when all reference to the departed being has been obliterated, this remnant—this echo, this keeper of a lost soul—remains and broods for, oh, a few millennia.

In the case of an entire burial ground such as once stood on this cliff-side land, a community of sad shades broods together, creating an atmosphere that draws other melancholy shades, in turn repulsing bright spirits and helpful angels. Such a deepening vortex of depressed energy attracts outright evil energy, the personality-disordered segment of the spirit world.

Over the next two hundred years, descendants of the original couple displayed a wide range of mental disorders: alcoholism, depression, aggression. Some of the luckier ones escaped this disturbing legacy by moving to the mainland or to other parts of the island. But certain of the ones who stayed to farm the property found themselves afflicted with bleak moods. Depression is contagious, after all. Think of an hour spent with a harsh, complaining person; even ten minutes in the company of a habitual pill can shatter our own good mood and trigger a flight response. So how much worse is it if we live with a legion of morose ghosts constantly whining and berating each other and us—even if it's all happening on an unconscious level?

We can only hope that as the dismal descendants of the cliff house settlers died off, many or even all of them merged into a realm of Love for the soul's cleansing. But the stain of their ill-will, sharp tempers, and sorrow hung over the property, swooping in and out to create a searing electromagnetic field—the kind that's strong enough to register on a ghost hunter's EMF meter.

In the 1860s a thirty-year-old whaling captain from New Bedford bought the land, tore down the slum of old farm shacks, and built for his beautiful nineteen-year-old bride a white clapboard Greek Revival cottage with aubergine shutters and picturesque gables. The captain went to sea for the following four years, and the young wife, although she missed him dearly, thrived in this setting. She may have sensed the surrounding sadness of the cliff side, but she had a strong character and set up an unconscious shield of light.

In the warm months she enriched the soil to cultivate flowers and vegetables. Her favorite animals were her three dogs and one affectionate goat named Evangeline, all of whom followed her on rambles along the cliffs and beaches. In the winter she walked to the village to teach reading and arithmetic to the children. Back at home she whistled, chattered to her pets, prepared hearty stews and aromatic pies, and stenciled everywhere she could find a bare piece of wall in the cottage.

In the years this radiant and loving woman presided over the house, the encircling sad phantoms withdrew to the edges of the property. A host of invisible guardians moved in to protect the young captain's wife, thus building up the good *geists* of the land. Had the woman's benevolent presence extended over the years and the coming generations, this cliff site might have been changed for the good. Instead, one sparkling day in September, the woman slipped on a section of the cliff eroded by a recent storm (or was she pushed?). She, Evangeline, and two of her dogs tumbled to the rocks below, and all were killed.

When her husband returned, his bereavement deepened during the time he spent in the honeymoon house. After he shipped out again, the property lay fallow for many years.

The negative vortex reopened.

In 1910 the tumble-down "haunted house" on the cliffs

was sold to a Boston Brahmin family who remodeled it in the new Arts & Crafts bungalow style. The father was cold and patriarchal, the mother dissatisfied and sour, the children growing into bitter people thanks to their parents' lack of tenderness. Their few weeks spent at the cliff house should have been summer idylls, but between their own family hostilities and the spirit world's message of menace, no one found pleasure there. At this point, flesh-and-blood beings and etheric energies were attracting heavier-duty percussions from a place of pure evil. The cliff house was openly haunted now, with dishes crashing in the night, unlit lamps combusting, and occasional gale-force winds churning through sealed rooms.

Once a cleaning girl from the village felt herself get pushed down the stairs. She survived the accident with no more than a twisted ankle, but some months later when a weekend guest, a Harvard professor with Puritan antecedents (and a puritanical personality of his own) fell down the stairs and died of a concussion, the maid wondered if he too had been pushed. *Must'a been,* she thought. *Too bad he hadn't lived to speak of it.* Or had he *died* to speak of it? After the tragedy, occupants of the house sometimes woke in the middle of the night to see the figure of a man in pajamas standing over them holding a candle and treating them to a fierce scowl.

And so it went, right up to the present and the new six-thousand-square-foot trophy house, whose owners divorced upon its completion, and whose only child, a freshman home from Brown University, committed suicide by jumping off the cliff not far from the spot where the captain's bride had fallen.

Hello, fresh new demons!

——

So, you see how the living and the dead are partners in making their own spot of the world into heaven or hell?

And some locations are haunted more by the living than the dead.

A few years back I rented a guest cottage with sloping ceilings and a pleasant view of the Oak Bluffs Harbor. With naval-grey painted subflooring, no windows to starboard and port, and downstairs bedrooms partitioned off with sheets of particle board, this rental had never been tenanted by anyone who considered it home. As a result, no one had ever stayed for more than a few months at a time. I figured I'd change all that. I'm a dab hand at decorating, so I moved in my own much-loved furniture and collection of antiques, my boon companions (a cat and a dog), and I lived happily ever after.

Well, not exactly.

I resided there for a full three years—a record for that cottage—but happiness eluded me. The family next door, a married couple with five kids, screeched at each other day and night. My neighbors on the other side—summer Vineyarders with grown kids and grandkids—were so unfriendly that at one point I knocked on their kitchen door and handed the husband a bouquet of flowers and a note suggesting we exchange a civil hello now and then. I'd written, "If we can't even *like* our neighbors as ourselves, where is our world going?" No response.

Even worse, the two cottages lined up directly behind me were deserted and steadily decaying into the ground, just like your classic haunted houses. Not once in three years did I see a light burning in those two dwellings.

Sometimes I would sit alone upstairs, gazing out at the lavender glow of sunset on the harbor, and I could positively feel the aches and pains of prior tenants. The landlady had told me they'd all been drug users and other varieties of losers. It hardly helped matters that, when his children weren't handy, the yelling dad next door picked fights with whoever lived in the guest cottage.

Were there ghosts in my house? Sometimes late at night, reading in my bedroom below, I heard footsteps treading the overhead floorboards. It made sense that the morose beings in the vicinity had attracted a random spirit. Or could the spirit have started it all, spoiling the outlook of anyone who happened to rent this cottage? My sense of the place was that the suffering humans who lived there affected each other more than an occasional roving ghost would have done. (I must confess that sometimes I wondered if the angry man and woman next door were possessed by minor demons.)

Bottom line: Most paranormally haunted houses aren't nearly as haunted as the cliffside cottage described earlier. In fact, the spirits might very well have a benign influence on the living. This goes to show that, while the living and the dead do indeed collaborate by contributing to the psychical pH of any given environment, human beings at their worst are more toxic than most denizens of the spirit world.

So, what's been assembled in the following chapters? More ghosts on this island (and in this region) than ever, some fun stuff, a hint of the path that connects the supernatural with the Divine, ghosts and people teaming up (willingly or unwillingly) in the world we share—all of it, ideally, propelling you, honored reader, on your own nascent ghost-hunting career.

THE
LAVENDER
ROOM

D ecember 2007. Most of the Victorian manor houses
of Ocean Park had been boarded up for the season.
As I studied them, their dark spires seemed to trail
off into the starry skies, onyx to the east and burgundy to the
west where the lights from town lightened the gloom. In the
center of the park, a ring of globed lamps shone around the
cold, white gazebo like the lonely moons of Jupiter. I snapped

a picture centered on the gazebo, and a galaxy of tiny lights showed up on my digital playback. Ghostly orbs, or merely an out-of-control read-out of reflections from the lamps?

You be the judge . . .

I was there that evening because I had been contacted by the owner of a particular house on Ocean Park Avenue. Arlen Westbrook, who resides in the Southwest, visits the Vineyard off-season. She has owned the property since 1962, but her new husband, who is older, finds traveling increasingly difficult, so her Vineyard time is limited.

Like many seasonal residents, Arlen has always rented her cottage to vacationers for a week here, two weeks there. Many of her tenants return year after year, even the ones who decided they enjoy a gentler holiday when they avoid the cottage's lavender bedroom.

I snapped nine pictures of the house on Ocean Park during my visit. Each angle disclosed a wealth of orbs of varying sizes. Some of the photographs looked as if Tinkerbell had flicked her wand to coat the house with pixie dust. I had never seen anything quite like it.

As a test, I retraced my steps and took pictures of all the neighboring cottages; not a speck of fairy shimmers turned up on any of them, although an occasional milky white orb appeared. This was Ocean Park, after all, where spirits of the past have long been know to waft in and out.

Arlen's tenants had mentioned odd doings at the cottage, and she asked them to jot down their memories of events. (Interestingly, when you consider all the people who hesitate to report a ghost for fear of sounding foolish, along with the scientific types who reflexively assert, "There must be a rational explanation!" you can safely formulate this ratio: For every person who reports a ghost at a particular property, two others have also experienced a paranormal incident there, but will never tell).

One of Arlen's tenants, a young man who wishes to

remain anonymous, wrote about an experience from a few
years back:

> My girlfriend was not too happy with me, so I
> had taken up residence in the lavender room. I woke
> up with the weird feeling that someone else was in
> the room. I looked toward the window and saw what
> looked like a small figure—a girl, probably, on the
> younger side. She just sat there looking down at the
> floor. I believe she had light-colored hair, probably
> blond. I think she was wearing a light blue or purple
> shirt. I thought it was my girlfriend, and decided to
> ignore her, as she was mad at me, so I went back to
> sleep. In the morning I asked her why she'd come
> into my room and sat there. She told me I was crazy,
> and that she had never entered the room that night.
> I'm sure I saw something, and if it wasn't her then . . .
> I don't know.

——

The second witness to the ghost in the lavender room
was a woman who recalled several peculiar occurrences:

> My friend and I had been renting the house
> on Ocean Park since 1984. My friend slept in the big
> bedroom to the right of the stairs. I slept in the bed-
> room over to the left.
>
> One night in the summer of 1992 I awoke and
> saw a woman in a wheelchair sitting at the foot of
> the bed. She looked like a real person, not a form
> made of mist. The wheelchair was old-fashioned
> with a caned back, and it looked as if the shadow of
> a man stood behind it, though I couldn't see any
> detail. I remember telling myself to look at the clock
> on the night-stand to see what time it was. It was
> 1:11 a.m. The woman looked to be in her seventies,
> had chin-length bobbed yellow-white hair, and wore

a long-sleeved black dress. I felt she was very angry at me for being there in the room. She wanted me out. I felt threatened.

She kept staring at me. She slowly lifted her skirt above her knees to show me her lower legs. They were chalk white, with golf-ball-sized lumps all over them, like some sort of calcification under the skin.

Through it all she just kept staring at me. I was too shocked to move and run to wake up my friend because the lady was blocking my getaway. I would have to go past or "through" her to get to the door. I was too scared to call out or say anything. So I turned around in bed, got on my knees, buried my face in my pillow, and prayed for the woman to disappear. I didn't look back to see if she had.

I awoke in the morning in the same position, on my knees with my face in the pillow.

After that I never slept in the lavender room again. And I never really liked being upstairs alone. In the following years we would talk to the ghost and tell her we were back, and we often closed the door to her room at night to leave her in peace.

The next summer on Ocean Park, we brought a Ouija board to see if we could contact the ghost. We asked who she was, and if we could contact her. All that was spelled out was "tktk tk tk."

Several years later, we again rented the house on Ocean Park. Soon after we arrived, a group of women showed up, believing they had reserved the cottage that week. We didn't have our lease with us, and one woman in the group became upset because she was convinced the house was hers. The atmosphere became very confrontational, with the same woman suggesting we let them stay there too, since there were lots of beds in the house. [Author's note: Our two protagonists should have put the entire group in the lavender room!]

We reached Arlen by phone and got the matter straightened out: my friend and I did indeed have the cottage for the week. We helped the other vacationers rent a vacant condo in the Tucker House, also on Ocean Park. We offered to lend them some extra blankets from our house. I went upstairs to the lavender room and took some blankets from the cabinet over the bed. As I started down the stairs, I felt two hands shove my back. I lost my balance and fell forward down the stairs. My friend was at the bottom and saw me fall. One foot took the brunt of it. The whole occurrence was so weird, I took a picture of my foot. It was black and blue, especially my big toe.

I felt that, at the time this happened, a lot of "bad vibes" had been stirred up in the house by the mix-up with the women. And maybe the ghost wasn't happy that I violated our agreement to stay out of her room.

In the summer of 2004, my sister came to stay with me at the house. She had been told about the ghost and, driven by curiosity, made a choice to sleep in the lavender room. I was sleeping in the big room across the hall when I heard a loud BAM! from the other room. I dashed into the room to find that, as she slept, my sister's arm had smashed hard against the wall. It frightened both of us, but the next day my sister suggested that perhaps she'd had an accident from tossing and turning in her sleep.

Many people ask my friend and me why we keep returning to the cottage. It's been our traditional vacation spot for many years. We love the house and have enjoyed grand times there, with many rich memories. And we haven't minded being respectful of whoever else might be staying there with us!

———

This intrepid tenant showed tremendous grace and good sportsmanship by ceding the bedroom over to the fuming ghost who—to give her her due—undoubtedly had no idea what this interloper was doing in her bed.

So how did the lavender room at an undisclosed location on Ocean Park become so packed with proprietary interest from the Other Side?

———

The lovely old cottage has housed its share of joys and sorrows. The house was constructed in the late 1860s after the Oak Bluffs Land and Wharf company sold the small lots on the grand park to affluent homeowners. A series of socially prominent families owned the cottage—the Reads, the Burroughses, the Sanbornes, the Bodfishes—though none of them held the deed for more than a few years. And none of the women in these families matches the description of the mad-as-hell apparition in the wheelchair, although, as I've pointed out before, any one of their spirits may also float through the house from time to time, driven by whatever small wedge of their psyches retains some nostalgia for the place.

Then we come to Harrah and Irene Bennett, who bought the cottage in 1925. Harrah was a popular Providence radio personality known as Uncle Red. The Bennetts spent many summers in the cottage and eventually moved in year-round. (The mountain of coal Arlen and her husband found in the basement when they bought the property attested to this.)

Bizarrely enough, in March of 1957 both Harrah and Irene fell seriously ill—from different ailments—at the same time. According to a *Vineyard Gazette* newspaper clipping, a son-in-law arrived from far away to deal with the joint crisis. In the handful of articles about the Bennetts, the usual requirement for a son-in-law, i.e., a daughter, is never mentioned, not even in the Bennetts' respective obituaries, which describe them as being "without heirs." As so often happens when we begin to delve for historical data, it's the absence of information that suggests a secret woe.

The no-longer-broadcasting Uncle Red died in 1958. Irene, after a long, debilitating illness in a Vineyard Haven nursing home, passed on in 1962, the year Arlen and Perry Westbrook acquired the cottage. If the ghost of Irene Bennett made an initial pass at her lavender bedroom instead of venturing forth to the Great Beyond, she might have begun a long period of discouragement to find it frequently occupied.

Arlen and Perry, their two adopted kids, and his three children from a previous marriage enjoyed the Ocean Park cottage for many happy summers. Perry died in 1998, and in 2002 Arlen married Marshall Clinard, a retired sociology professor.

One final piece of family history is included because it may contribute to the spirit content of the Ocean Park cottage: Arlen's daughter, Joyce, of Native American heritage, died at the age of twenty-eight. Her own cherished, private domain during her family's summer vacations was the lavender room.

———

On a frigid night in mid-December of 2007, I visited the seasonally dark and brooding cottage on Ocean Park with my buddies Bob Alger, Bob Kent, and Patrick MacAllister from the Pilgrim Paranormal Research Group. Arlen had mailed me a key and her blessings. The men heaped their equipment on the kitchen table and switched on a battery-operated lantern. In a few more minutes they had their electromagnetic field meter in hand, carrying it from room to room to arrive at a baseline reading of 0.1. A thermometer recorded forty-seven degrees, but it dipped into the high twenties as the evening wore on. Electronic voice recorders were activated in strategic locations.

All three men strapped red lights to their foreheads, the better to reduce visual interference, both to the naked eye and the camera. Their cold streams of breath turned from silver to ruby red.

Bob A. announced our arrival in each room with a friendly "Hello" and an assurance that we were here on a brief visit. We all made mention of thumps and bumps as these sounds occurred; sometimes only one of us heard a noise, other times we noted it together. At one point Bob K. remarked, peering up to the pointed ceiling of the front bedroom, "I heard a male voice, maybe coming through the vent?"

But it was in the lavender room that things started to get lively.

We'd drifted in and out of the tiny, high-ceilinged bedroom several times until finally we focused on a framed portrait of a dark-haired Victorian debutante. All of a sudden the space we stood in grew colder, going from refrigerator chilly to the swirling mists of meat-locker cold. The electromagnetic field meter, which had remained at the baseline 0.1 now spiked to 0.3. Then as we continued to gaze at the portrait, something kicked the inside of the closet door, hard and loud.

Suddenly I remembered I was up past my bedtime and announced that I was heading home.

Bob, Bob, and Patrick stayed for a couple more hours to continue their investigation. A week later, Bob A. e-mailed me:

> In the middle bedroom upstairs we heard a
> girl's voice—unintelligible, though we picked up a
> definite "Hi"—we caught it on the audio of one of
> the video cameras. Shortly after that, the EM meter
> in the violet room alarmed. Bob also got a picture
> in the front bedroom of a mist forming. Also there
> were a couple of times when we were out of the
> house, warming up in the truck, when the EM meter
> alarmed. We heard a lot of footsteps, and a lot of
> banging noises that could have been a loose shutter;

it's hard to say. There seemed to be more bangs and noises when we were out of the house; [the ghosts] were shy when we were inside with them. All in all, an interesting night."

———

Amen to that.

Some weeks later, when Bob and his crew were cleaning up the audio of the disembodied girl's voice, they were able to tease out this message: "You're probably looking for me."

CONFEDERATES ON PEDESTALS

If you read the *Vineyard Gazette* (or any of the smaller, long-gone island newspapers of the nineteenth century) on microfiche, covering the years of 1860 to 1865, you would scarcely know the Civil War was going on. Camp meeting picnics, moonlit wagon rides to South Beach, and the new rage for croquet commanded greater attention from the local reading public. Vineyarders have always had an absolute libido for denial, and it's easy enough to nurture this pathology on any island without a bridge to the mainland, where all the serious stuff is happening.

Even in the decades preceding the Civil War, the pressing issue of slavery was, embarrassingly enough in hindsight, a source of ambivalence on the Vineyard. Slavery was illegal here, but that was because it had long before been banned in Boston. A purely poisonous piece of federal legislation had come along in 1793, the Fugitive Slave Act, compelling citizens in antislavery states to remand escaped slaves to their owners. Then the Commonwealth of Massachusetts, bless its heart, before the election of 1860, passed the Personal Liberty Act, obstructing that vile law and allowing runaways the right to plead their case before a jury.

Some Vineyarders helped these fugitives by hiding them among the more accepting mixed-ancestry residents of Gay Head, or by escorting them on the next leg of their journey, to New Bedford. From there, the escaped slaves would go on to Boston and then to safety in Canada.

And this, too, was good: Vineyarders voted for Abraham Lincoln in larger proportions than did townsfolk anywhere else in the nation. But events heated up faster than wise minds could take stock: South Carolina seceded from the Union, six more states followed, forming the Confederacy; Fort Sumter was fired on and federal troops were sent to intervene; eight more states seceded, and the cannons were rolled out.

If Mr. Lincoln could have spent a few days with island locals, his long legs stretched across a Campground porch rail, he might have been prevailed upon to try diplomacy before killing off hundreds of thousands of his citizens. (Mark Kurlansky, in his 2006 book *Nonviolence*, demonstrates convincingly how the battle could have been averted, and emancipation achieved, without unleashing the dogs of war.)

At the war's start, *Gazette* editor Edgar Marchant invited publishers and politicians around the nation to let go of their antagonisms and come fishing on the Vineyard: "If they are terribly pugnacious and excited, let them go out and harpoon sharks, and bang them on the head with a good-sized club."

Island dwellers are accidental utopians in that they have rarely, if ever, been crusaders, which means they haven't added to the world's woes. Let us take care of our own plot of ground; you're welcome to join us, but don't ask us to join you—that, in a nutshell, is the unspoken policy of island living.

During the Civil War years, one could see this live-and-let-live approach play itself out every time a new call for volunteers and, later, draftees, came down from the state capital. Virtually no Vineyarder signed up. Most able-bodied men could find an exemption that fit their circumstances (sole surviving son, sole support of a wife and children, etc.). Failing a good, juicy exemption, or the very solid excuse of absence at sea, anyone could buy his ticket out with a three-hundred-dollar bounty paid to a professional recruiter in Boston who hired substitute recruits (often recently arrived Irish immigrants). Many of these recruits for hire would sign up, desert, and sign up again under a new name to collect another bounty.

At town meetings on the Vineyard, voters authorized bonds to pay the bounties for the men who would *not* be marching off to war. Let us not forget that, in spite of what our third-grade social studies classes taught us, no one in the North was asked to fight to end slavery. Lincoln strongly believed that soldiers would lay down their arms and desert in droves if *that* were the rallying cry. Rather, they were fighting to preserve the Union. At this juncture, the states had been "united" for a mere eighty-five years.

———

After the war, the new editor of the *Gazette*, James Cooms, Jr., took advantage of his new bully pulpit to write: "The future historian will point to the leaders of the rebellion as being the indirect cause of the abolition of slavery on this continent—showing how good is made to spring out of evil."

(What Cooms did here was give Confederates the credit for ending slavery in spite of themselves. This is twisted thinking but it is also, somehow, very Vineyard.)

And so life continued on apace, with the usual byproduct of war: recession and grievances nursed for generations on both sides of the conflict. On the Vineyard, animosities were muted, though not entirely lacking. As usual there were more pressing local concerns—a bad economy, not enough jobs, too few amusements, rampant alcohol use—so what else is new? But in this Yankee stronghold very little Monday morning quarterbacking was going on about the late war. That is, until 1891, when Charles Strahan, Oak Bluffs newspaper publisher and veteran of the 21st Virginia Regiment, decided to erect a monument to an unidentified Civil War solider. Originally located at the base of Circuit Avenue, it was moved in the early twentieth century to its present site facing the Sound on a triangle of lawn above Ocean Park.

Let me put into the record here that this bronze statue has always been known colloquially as the Confederate Soldier. It's been painted blue. It's been painted grey. Numerous times. It's even been green, due to oxidation of the metal.

It's still referred to as the Confederate Soldier, although island historians will correct you until they're blue (or grey or green) in the face.

No one knew quite what Mr. Strahan had in mind when he paid a small fortune for the statue. Was he trying to sneak a Rebel into a Yank town? Mr. Strahan insisted the monument was designed to end all lingering hostilities, and to celebrate peace, glorious peace.

Yet somehow the feeling remains that we've got Confederates in the attic (to borrow from the title of Islander Tony Horowitz's hilarious book). We've certainly got Confederates on the sea. Mr. Robert Douglas, founder of the Black Dog tavern, tee-shirt, and souvenirs empire, maintains two exquisite nineteenth-century reproduction schooners in the Vineyard

Haven harbor, the *Shenandoah* and the *Alabama*. The original schooners bearing these names belonged to Southern privateers and were responsible for decimating New England's whaling fleet during the Civil War. These Rebel swashbucklers routinely captured civilian ships, dumped the mariners ashore, then set fire to the vessels. A good half-dozen Vineyard whalers were destroyed in this manner.

Surprisingly, we've also got ghostly remnants of grey-clad soldiers on our porches.

———

I was keeping my parapsychologist's eye on a particular cottage in the Campground after a man in his early fifties paid a visit to me in my bookstore in the summer of 2003. He and his wife had recently purchased a house alongside the charming white parish hall, a Campground landmark that resembles a church in a tiny Vermont village. The weekend before the man's visit to my store, the couple had come up to their new home to take stock.

He sensed immediately that something was not right with their house. A great many things were not right. Objects toppled from shelves. Small items such as a spatula or a sink-side sponge would disappear, then reappear precisely where they were supposed to be. At one point, the new homeowner watched, aghast, as a beaded-glass salt shaker slid across the breakfast table without the help of any visible human hand. Then the pepper shaker followed suit, clinking alongside its companion.

"The funny part of all of this," he said, "was that I couldn't discuss it with my wife. She's a scientist, with all the skepticism that comes with that profession. If I said anything about ghosts to her, she'd bite my head off!"

When it came time to pack up and leave at the end of the weekend, an unmistakable tension had developed between the pair. They were silent on the ferry passage, and the silence continued during the car ride north out of Wood's Hole and up Route 28 toward Boston. Not until they had glided up and over the soaring heights of the Bourne Bridge, and left Cape Cod behind, did his wife turn to him and say, "Shall we talk about the ghost?"

I asked the beleaguered new homeowner to keep me updated, but several years elapsed without my hearing another word from him. As part of my research, I added the cottage—grey shingles, cream and Pompeian-red jigsaw trim, yellow shutters—to my list of potentially haunted houses, which meant it received a long, searching glance whenever I walked past it.

Three years later, I could tell that something was still amiss with this cottage. A telltale indication of paranormal activity is a house sitting dark and unused. I'm not talking about a derelict, abandoned house—that, of course, is a blatant sign. So is a house on Martha's Vineyard in a highly desirable location, in fine fettle, standing unlit and vacant, with the owners disinclined to rent it for big bucks or lend it to friends or family. It needn't be anything overt—no spooks leaping from broom closets or creepy moans issuing from the basement. Instead, there might be something in the very atmosphere of the house that makes the occupants anxious or depressed, but they never for a moment place the blame on the spirit world. Instead they simply find reasons to go elsewhere for the summer, and feel no motivation to share their strangely unwonderful house with loved ones.

And so it was, or seemed to be, with this cottage.

Then, one late afternoon in August, I was ambling up from the harbor with Huxley on his leash. From one of the tiny connecting lanes, lined chock-a-block with gingerbread mini-palaces, we entered the main circle called Trinity Park and, in the distance, I glimpsed a man seated on the porch of the cottage by the pretty, white parish hall.

At last, someone using the house!

The man was perched on a rocking chair at the far end

of the veranda. He was leaning forward, hands on his knees, feet planted firmly on the boards, legs together. I saw to my amazement he was dressed in a Civil War uniform, specifically a Confederate uniform: white, long-sleeved shirt with a slender grey band at the high collar, a grey billed cap on his head. Must be going to a costume party, I thought.

By the time I was within twenty feet of the porch, I noticed that he was sitting improbably still and that his skin tone was dull, a deep, unnatural beige.

You dope! I chided myself. He's a mannequin! My next words to myself were: But just in case he's not a mannequin, stop staring! It's rude!

Let me add that the man never once looked at me, so if I stared, chances were I wasn't provoking him with my lack of courtesy. Instead, he was gazing straight ahead, as if he were watching the antics of children or dogs at play in the park.

Trying to keep my own gaze straight ahead, I walked past him, Huxley at my heels. Then my curiosity got the better of me because, well, I sensed that something important was taking place. I turned for one last look.

At this point, the figure should have been seated only about three feet behind me. Only he wasn't. He was gone.

So was the rocking chair.

I stopped. So did Huxley. He crooked his ears in different directions—his way of indicating he had no idea what I was trying to tell him. (Unlike some canines, Huxley seems to be unfazed by—or oblivious to—ghosts.) He stared at me with his beady, buggy, Boston terrier eyes.

"Huxley, I think we've just seen a ghost."

If anyone had caught me talking out loud to my dog, I might have looked pretty beady and buggy myself.

PUTTIN' ON
THE RITZ, AT YOUR
OWN RISK

In May 2006, a couple of Boston University girls down for the Memorial Day weekend had a brush with the supernatural in a honky-tonk cafe. I can almost hear the late Rod Serling's solemn voice as he narrates the girls' experience: "A dark night on a haunted island, a jukebox playing a forgotten tune, and two young women who are about to meet a barfly from . . . the Twilight Zone."

The Ritz Cafe, near the bottom eastern corner of Circuit Avenue, may not be Oak Bluffs' oldest saloon, but it's arguably the funkiest, loudest, grittiest, and most colorful dive on the entire island. Only the biggest night-owls and the most continuously inebriated locals frequent the Ritz Cafe. "Everybody knows your name," applies to Ritz regulars as much as it does to the more upscale clientele of the Cheers bar on television, but at the Ritz everyone also knows you drink Cutty Sark shots with beer chasers.

For all its hard-drinking atmosphere, the old watering hole is not so scary that you're likely to get pummeled if you root for the wrong baseball team. On the contrary, the Ritz is nothing short of cozy. Excellent bands often play there—island favorites such as Johnny Hoy and the Bluefish and the Sultans of Swing. A second room holds an elderly pool table. Locals waiting for take-out pizza at Giordano's feel comfortable hanging out in this quieter room, pool cue in hand, able to absorb some of the fellowship from a distance.

The building began as a fish market in 1872, some years later changing over to a fruit and confectioner business, followed by an ice cream parlor. During the 1920s and 30s a package store held pride of place, but the Ritz has been the Ritz since 1944, and we're all better off for it.

On one notable occasion, April Fool's Day 1997, the Ritz's management hosted a special marriage ceremony. Any amorous couple could step forward to be wed for the night, no questions asked about alternate spousal commitments. Local blues singer Gordon Healy hitched up the temporary brides and grooms, who, along with their guests, danced until closing time. One of the Just Married couples won the raffle for a getaway weekend at the none-too-plush Surfside Motel, down the way and across the street.

When the Ritz was undergoing renovations in the early 1980s and had to shut down for a month, islanders observed that a bevy of parked cars kept turning up every evening in the normally deserted parking lot of the East Chop Beach Club. The deal was, if you couldn't drink in good company, you could always BYOB and pile into a car with some buddies. An island wag called it "the Ritz *Sur Mer.*" The ocean view was free of charge.

———

Yes, nearly every Vineyarder under ninety has stepped into the Ritz Cafe at least once.

Their first visit was also fated to be their last for the two Boston University students, Blaine* (19), and Kaitlyn* (20). The girls possessed the rite-of-passage fake IDs to allow just this sort of bar sortie.

On the night in question, the two pretty girls—Blaine with shoulder-length auburn hair and Kaitlyn with pale blonde hair pulled back and clasped with a tortoise-shell barrette—wore low-scooped tank tops, designer denim shorts and, respectively, hot pink and turquoise Crocs. It was about seven o'clock in the evening, and the girls pointedly avoided the gaze of the male regulars who were already on their way to getting sloppily drunk. Even without eye contact, the girls could feel urgent, bemused stares streaming in their direction.

It required no more than a rudimentary knowledge of human nature to know the guys *had* to be thinking, What are these hotties doing here?!

The girls turned to face the bartender, a plump, mid-forties woman with a shag of dark hair. Blaine ordered a *mojito,* Kaitlyn a glass of white wine. When their drinks arrived, they continued to stand and face the white vinyl counter and the shelves of bottles on the wall behind the bar. Nonetheless, they felt fervid stares boring into their backs.

Kaitlyn took a sip of her wine, then jerked her head around. "Someone just tapped my shoulder!" she said to Blaine.

Blaine took a long searching look around the room. "The closest person is ten feet away," she said.

Kaitlyn shrugged, then set her glass on the counter. "Big mistake coming here."

"Let's finish up our drinks and find someplace to eat."

The blonde nodded, relaxing her shoulders. But then she let out a low cry and spun her head around again. "Goddammit!"

"What?"

"I got tapped again!" Now it was Kaitlyn's turn to take a long look at the faces in the bar. She thought they showed expressions of fake innocence.

Blaine felt a flare of impatience. "Look, I'm right next to you. Wouldn't I notice if someone snuck up and touched you?"

Kaitlyn sighed and belted back the rest of her wine. Her expression was so sour that her friend said with a laugh, "Look, I'll take a picture with my cell phone the minute you sound off again. At least I can prove there's no one messing with you."

For a few moments Kaitlyn stared blankly into her friend's upheld camera as Blaine, with her free hand, took a long pull on her *mojito*.

All of a sudden Kaitlyn let out a piercing scream and clapped a hand to her right eyeball. Instinctively, Blaine snapped a picture at the same instant.

The bar had gone from a high-decibel chatter to silence, although now the jukebox sounded extra loud as it wailed, "Born on the Bay-ou! Born on the Bay-ou, baby!" All attention was centered on Kaitlyn as she covered her eye with both hands.

"Someone scratched my eye!"

Blaine gently lifted her friend's hand away from her face and, tilting up her chin, peered at her with concern.

Kaitlyn's eye was red, and it flowed with tears of injury. Then both eyes shed tears as she cried at the shock and pain.

Blaine examined the screen on her cell phone to see who was responsible for the attack. In the digital image, no one lurked anywhere near Kaitlyn. But what the camera *had* captured was a jagged white streak of liquid light, about three feet in length, and streaming toward Kaitlyn's right eye.

———

After hearing about this experience, whenever I've had the opportunity—or the nerve—to ask a Ritz regular about ghost stories, he or she invariably says the living customers routinely kick up too much of a ruckus for them to notice anything more, well, nuanced going on from the spirit world. (Then, invariably, they add a secondary but enthusiastic comment: "The music's awesome!") All the same, I *have* picked up the following paranormal tidbits.

An attractive blonde in her forties told me, "One night three years ago, there was this handsome dude—blue eyes, sort of bald in that cool, shaved way—at the bar. He knew my name before I told him, though I was pretty hammered, so maybe I told him! Anyway, he talked to me—he was so serious!—about what a bummer it was to drink too much. He made such an impression on me, I've been sober ever since— swear to God! And the funny thing is, I never saw him before, and I haven't run into him since! Not once! I think he was a guardian angel!"

A middle-aged male Harley rider reports having fallen off the same barstool four or five times. "It's the one at the far end near the door. And I drink mostly ginger ale, so I wonder if there's this mean drunk Ritz ghoul that keeps shoving me!"

Barroom ruckus or bad-boy ghosts? Aside from the eye-scratching episode, a visit to the Ritz promises to be more pleasurable than paranormal.

And the music *is* awesome!

RANDOM
GHOSTS
I

M y favorite cab company is Martha's Vineyard Taxi,
partly because I have its phone number memo-
rized—not an easy accomplishment once one is
past a certain age—and mostly because Morgan, the twenty-
eight-year-old, red-headed company owner, sometimes brings
his Portuguese water dog, Manny, along for the ride.

One drizzly night last November, I called Morgan for a

ride home after attending a play at the Katharine Cornell Theater in Vineyard Haven.

"I've been meaning to tell you something," he said when he pulled up, looking a little sheepish. "This vehicle we're driving maybe has a ghost. Two of my drivers last summer started to get upset about it."

A young woman to whom he'd assigned the gently used SUV (only twenty thousand miles on it when he bought it from an off-island dealer), was the first to get spooked. On her after-midnight runs, after she'd dropped off her fare and was alone in the cab, if she glanced in the rear-view mirror she'd catch sight of the shadowy outline of a man positioned in the center of the seat behind her.

"If I'd reached between the front seats I could have touched his lap," she told Morgan. "That's how close he was."

The first time it happened, she gave a cry and turned around to look, but saw no one there. After a while she refused to drive that particular vehicle. Other problems arose, and eventually Morgan had to let her go. Shortly thereafter the erstwhile taxi driver left the island.

"The funny part was," Morgan said to me, "she passed on her fears to one of the guys who worked for me. He swore up and down he'd seen this backseat rider too. He'd get this feeling of not being alone in the car, and—sure enough—he'd peek in the mirror and see this guy in the back seat."

(In an amusing twist, one night this same driver dropped off a bunch of young tipplers at a house in Katama. Unbeknownst to him, one of the gang had passed out on the floor of the rear seat. When the fellow later revived enough to throw an arm over the seat back and let out a loud gurgle, the driver shouted in terror and swerved the cab over to the side of the road.)

Morgan and I speculated about the history of the taxi as he drove me home. Could someone have been murdered in it? I suggested. Died of a heart attack while bumping along to an undisclosed location? It reminded me of my favorite Emily Dickinson lines:

> Because I could not stop for Death,
> He kindly stopped for me;
> The carriage held but just ourselves
> And Immortality.

Apparently Morgan had already wondered about the vehicle's provenance too, but had found it was impossible to track its background in detail: "It was used for its first twenty thousand miles as a rental car. Hundreds of people drove it."

"Did the dealer drop any hints about a, um, problem?"

"Why would he? I know I wouldn't!"

Naturally a conversation such as this provokes you, almost against your will, to glance at the back seat. There was no one there. For the moment.

———

As you'll see, this one is and isn't a ghost story . . .

A house called the Silo sits all by itself on a beach on Chappaquiddick's southwest shore. Its name is derived from the short, squat tower enclosing the sole bedroom. A picture window occupies the length of the wall of the living room which, predictably, overlooks a deck and the sparkling expanse of Katama Bay. Providing they don't mind having to shove the two twin beds together, the Silo is a perfect place for an amorous couple to enjoy some romantic time to themselves with only sea and sky for company.

A man in his early to mid-thirties named Billy* rented the Silo for a week in July 1994. In those days I worked for a real estate company in Edgartown, and I was the agent who hooked Billy up with his Chappy rental. He told me his girlfriend would be accompanying him, which made me glad for him, considering the Silo's private setting. Next he mentioned that his parents would join the party, which seemed to put a crimp in the week's enjoyment quotient but, as the French people say, *chacun à son goût* . . .

A couple of weeks after Billy's vacation had come and gone, he called me at the real estate office and said, "I have a couple of weird stories for you about the Silo, but you're going to think I'm loony-tunes."

By then I'd collected enough ghost stories (my first book, *Haunted Island,* was about to be published), that I recognized the symptons. He wasn't calling me to complain about the dust bunnies under the sofa.

He added hesitantly, "There may be a ghost."

"You're talking to the right person," I assured him.

He reported that on the first night of the rental the four of them had dinner at home. His parents, to whom he'd given the bedroom, called it an early night. Billy and his girlfriend would be sleeping on the pull-out sofa in the living room.

The bedroom had two single beds banked against opposite walls across a creaky, wood-planked floor. A tired old dresser sat between the beds. (The Silo was supremely rustic; the bathroom had a sink and toilet, but the shower, rusty spigots and all, stood in a warped enclosure outdoors. Lots of Vineyard houses have outdoor showers, but that doesn't preclude them having at least one shower indoors.)

The following morning, Billy's mother told him that she and his father had dozed off quickly, but sometime later she was awakened by the sound of someone treading across the floor boards. There was no moonlight coming in through the windows that evening, and of course there are no streetlights, so the room was dark as a bank vault. She assumed her husband was approaching to keep her company.

She felt and heard the mattress press down on the edge of her bed. She scooted over to make room just as she felt the sheet and blanket lifted back. The mattress sagged as a body stretched out alongside her. But she felt no body heat, no contact whatsoever.

She waited for a cuddle, but none was forthcoming.

"Ed?" she whispered into the dark, realizing at nearly the same instant that she could hear no sound beside her, certainly not her husband's slightly labored breathing. "Hey!" she said with a trace of asperity. No response.

She reached above the bed to switch on the cheap lamp clumsily nailed to the wall above her bed. A flood of light glared in the small bedroom.

There was no one in bed with her.

Furthermore, her husband was fast asleep on the mattress across the room. He lay on his side, facing away from her, his nighttime adenoidal breaths issuing from both his mouth and nose.

Billy paused for effect, then continued, "An even stranger thing happened a few nights later.

"It was Saturday night, and my parents had taken the car over to Edgartown on the little ferry. My girlfriend and I lounged around the Silo, grilled bluefish on the deck, watched the sunset from the living room, and then we got a little friendly on the sofa. I had my arm around her, and I happened to look up at the picture window. Just outside, I saw this chick in a long white dress *staring* at us! She raised her hand and waved. Then she stepped back and disappeared!

"At the time I didn't think there was anything supernatural about it. In fact I was steamed! Someone had come along to mess with our privacy! The only way out of the house was through the rear door, so I stomped out back and raced around to the deck to chew her out, whoever she was. She was gone. I looked both ways up and down the beach and, I'm telling you, there's no way a human being could have booked it out of there so fast that I wouldn't have seen her white dress waving in the wind."

This sounded very interesting from the point of view of ghost hunting. I told Billy I'd call the homeowners, find out about the Silo's history, and get back to him.

I hung up the phone and regaled my three office mates

with the tale of Billy's Excellent Chappy Adventure. One of my colleagues was Lynda Hathaway, the company bookkeeper. Lynda is a multigenerational islander with thick, brunette shoulder-length hair, a pretty, round face, and a lively sense of fun. At that moment, however, she had a funny expression on her face; all the highjinx had drained out of her. After the others had returned to their paperwork and phone calls, Lynda approached my desk, still looking a little green under the gills.

She said, "I was the lady in white."

It turned out that Lynda had gone to school with Billy. She knew he was vacationing here because he'd called and asked her to recommend a rental agent. She steered him my way.

On the Saturday night in question, Lynda was attending a party at the house of her brother, artist Dana Gaines, just a short jog up the beach. Around nine o'clock she thought about Billy. He'd confided that he and his wife (whom she also knew from school days) had recently separated. He'd sounded sad, and she worried that he was sitting alone in his remote little beach house feeling sorry for himself. The remedy for this, she determined, was for her to sprint along the shore and invite sad Billy to the party.

"I had on a white cotton blouse and white cotton skirt," she told me. "When I peered in the window to see if Billy was home, I saw him making out with this girl on the sofa! 'Well! He hasn't wasted any time!' I thought. When he looked up, I waved, but I was irked and embarrassed, so I ran like a madwoman back to Dana's. I guess Billy was wrong about me not having enough time to clear out of there."

I must confess, I was disappointed to learn that the story had what skeptics call a rational explanation. But in the next moment, I looked Lynda squarely in the eye and said, "Okay, but was it you who got into bed with his mom?"

———

When a ghost story is indistinguishable from an

appointment with guardian angels, one's entire life and philosophy can be altered.

In 1979, Janice Belisle, native Edgartownian, wife, and mother of a six-year-old daughter, was grieving for her father, who had recently died. Her daily rituals and obligations kept her going, however, and one of them was to teach religious classes at the Catholic parish hall on Pease Point Way, across from the Edgartown fire station.

"I had to drop something off one afternoon when I knew the church was empty," she told me. "I stood downstairs in the dark. It was so quiet you could hear the hallway clock ticking. And then all of a sudden I heard women singing upstairs. Normally this wouldn't be anything out of the ordinary—the big loft space was where we held choir practice. But there was no sign of human presence—no coats thrown on hooks or benches, no lights on anywhere."

The sound of singing was surreal. Janice mounted the stairs to find the vocalists. As she drew closer to the upstairs landing, she was aware of a heightened, unearthly quality to the psalm, unrecognizable but beautiful. The choir had never sounded so practiced, so . . . perfect. At the top of the stairs, Janice could see directly into the upper loft space. The room was empty. And yet voices spilled all around her, the acoustics of the hall amplifying the sweetness of the vocals.

When Janice recently told me about this experience, her eyes grew misty as she scrolled up the memory. "I've always thought my dad's spirit sent me this band of singing angels."

I mulled this over, then volunteered my own opinion: "I believe your dad may have facilitated it, but I'm thinking it couldn't have happened if you weren't scheduled in this lifetime for a state of grace. This one lasted for maybe an hour, maybe a few days, but it's changed you, hasn't it? It's opened your heart and given you a deeper sense of spiritual possibility?"

She nodded with a relieved smile. "I haven't told many people about this."

I sighed. "I know. If we could all share these events more openly, we'd create a gorgeous new world for ourselves."

Now it was Janice's turn to sigh. "It *was* a gorgeous experience."

"Your first," I said with a conviction that surprised me. "It won't be your last."

—

I've been keeping my eye on another Campground cottage in addition to the one that yielded the Confederate soldier. In June 2006, my friend, writer Jessica Harris (of Oak Bluffs, Queens, New York, and New Orleans), introduced me to her friend, Jana Napoli, also of New Orleans, who Jessica assured me was a true medium.

Jana, a short, dark woman with the shape of a pre-Columbian Earth Mother, said she'd love to attend my Oak Bluffs ghost tour one day because she'd encountered her own roster of spirits on her yearly visits to the island.

"The creepiest one is in the Campground. You know that little street that feeds in from the Oyster Bar and Grill? Just where it intersects the circular street around the Tabernacle, there's this grey-shingled cottage with orange and white trim. It's got a wraparound veranda, and facing the front, there's a . . . a presence. It's an old-time hellfire and brimstone preacher. The guy's way, way too intense."

"What's the matter with him?"

She shuddered. "He's always ranting as if he's still in the pulpit. He yells at all the people strolling by—not that they can hear him—but he tells them they're sinners and going straight to Hell! I mean, can you believe his nerve? All these nice, happy tourists going by, snapping pictures of these pretty little cottages, and this freak is blasting them?!" She let out a grim chortle. "These days I give a wide berth to that particular corner."

I wasn't surprised. This was a cottage where, way back during my first visit on a late November afternoon in 1977,

I'd seen a rocking chair tipping forward and back all by itself, while all the other rockers left out on Campground verandas sat perfectly still.

Jana Napoli told me her story at the start of the summer during which I later encountered the ghost of the Confederate soldier. You'll recall that the soldier's cottage had sat dark and deserted until that fateful August afternoon. So had this other house with the spirit of Cotton Mather on the porch. In this historic fantasyland, for *two* summer homes to stand idle must have constituted a record. Naturally, I decided this second Victorian dollhouse must also contain some serious ecto-life.

One Friday evening in July, as I entered the Campground with my ghost-walk group, I told them about the spirit of the fuming minister, pointing out the location up ahead on our left. As we flocked by the dark house—at about 8:15, so the sun had set and shadows were rife—a jagged bar of light sparked below the porch ceiling. It looked as if a fluorescent tube had slipped free of its metal pins and exploded in midair.

As a group, we jumped, cried "Eeek!" and asked each other, "What was that?!" I surely didn't know. I shook my head and we kept on walking.

The very next Friday night, I told another tour group what the other group had witnessed the week before. As we paraded up alongside the mad preacher's cottage, again, pitch black inside, a sonic boom like thunder erupted under our feet.

More jumps, more *eeek*s, more questions. Again I shook my head and we kept on walking.

Perhaps the crazed preacher, in those two successive Fridays, finally got his fury at us sinners out of his system, because no similar events occurred during my later tours. By the following summer, people were back living in the cottage, their lamps aglow each night.

As Julian of Norwich famously said, *"All shall be well, and all shall be well, and all manner of things shall be well."*

IN THE REALM OF THE PSYCHONATURAL

A nyone who does research into the paranormal—and sticks her neck out even further by writing about it— receives calls from people wanting an exorcism of their home. And often the people stand in dire need of exorcism themselves. It's not that they are possessed by demons, although I've met a few individuals who seem to go beyond any diagnosis of abnormal psychology, straight to the category of minion of the Devil. Still, when people think dark spirits lurk within their walls, creating depression, madness, accidents, and just plain doggone bad luck, chances are the occupants of the house, both living and dead, are contributing equally to the pool of misery.

When matters are past the point where a priest's holy water or a witch's wand will do any good whatsoever, I've had to recommend the Nadler Method, but we'll get to that later on.

The saddest case I've come across was presented to me in the fall of 2007 (and please note that I've changed the names and identities of the persons in the story because we live on a small island, and I hesitate to cause any undue chagrin).

A strikingly handsome man of about forty appeared in my bookstore one morning in late August. He introduced himself not by his own name but as the son of the late actor Graham Thomas, a movie star long connected with the island. My visitor's own name, as he told me secondarily, was Adam Thomas. His mother was equally famous: Claire Juneau, an expatriate playwright who lives in Madrid, but is often photographed at society functions in Manhattan.

Children of the celebrated seem to generally accept— and even to exploit—their reflected glory, but they seldom, if ever, seem truly happy. Adam was fine and dandy that day, however. He had the long, lanky physique and artlessly fab posture of the fashion model he'd been in his younger days. He wore designer jeans, a snug-fitting green Jellyfish shirt from the trendy new shop next door to mine, and his coifed brown hair, clean-cut and chiseled features, and sparkling turquoise eyes gave him a look of glamour and health.

"My house is in Katama," he told me, referring to the wide, open plain near the white sands of South Beach. "It's only seven years old, but it must have been built over a slew of old Indian bones. There's something inside it that's keeping me, my kids, my guests, my help, on pins and needles. Can you come look at it and suggest a remedy?"

We played desultory telephone tag over the course of two and a half months before finally settling on a mutually agreeable time for me to visit the house on a Monday in late November. I woke up that morning at five o'clock with a rip-roaring headache that I knew from experience would last until nightfall. I called Adam, and he said he too was "feeling sorry for" himself, having bumped his head on his parakeet's cage: "My eye has been bleeding and bleeding and *bleeding!*"

We changed our appointment to the same time, next day.

Feeling much better on Tuesday, I decided to rack my bike on the bus to Edgartown and then pedal the several miles down Katama Road to Adam's house. In a movie version of this story, my path would have been plagued by all sorts of obstacles and portents. Nothing fearsome actually occurred during my journey that day, but still, there was an indefinable sense of the fates shooing me back.

First, when I tried to wheel my bike from behind my building, it stubbornly resisted. I bent down to find a yellow bungie cord snagged in the spokes, and it took a good deal of prodding and prying to get it loose. Then, as I pointed the bike between the buildings, I found the narrow alleyway clogged by a fallen tree limb—odd, since there'd been no wind-storm the night before. I dragged the limb away and leaned it up against the trash cans. Once I was finally astride my bike and pedaling toward the bus stop, a sudden gust of wind blew in from the sea and nearly knocked me down, almost seeming to warn me to turn back.

Later, as I rolled along Katama Road, I realized Adam had been *non compos mentis* the day he'd dictated directions to me over the phone. I ended up about three-quarters of the way down the beach road and nowhere near a house, haunted or otherwise. The nearest structure was a grain silo in the middle of a field. I phoned Adam, gave him my coordinates, and asked whether I was *anywhere* near his home.

There was a long pause. Then he turned from the phone

to speak to someone in the room with him, saying, "Could you please explain to this lady how you got here today?"

Next I heard the breathy voice of a young woman who, it turned out, had been hired as his personal assistant that very morning. (Apparently Adam went through a great number of helpers. His employees regularly quit because Adam was (a) too demanding—his dog-walker would be told to make him breakfast, his assistant ordered to drive him to New York—and (b) notorious for not paying people. That day's unsuspecting young assistant gave me superb directions to her new employer's house, and I arrived inside of ten minutes.

The house was typical of the area—a hulking, shingled, reverse contemporary, which meant the living area was situated on the second floor, the better to take in the distant grey-blue line of ocean (about the best you can do for a water view on this part of the island). A sign on the red-enameled front door read, *If you can't be nice, go away.*

I reflected on this, as most visitors must have done, and decided I presented no problem.

A small, frail-looking man of about sixty answered the door. He had watery blue eyes, thinning and improbably yellow hair, and was dressed in grey flannel slacks, brown loafers, and a button-down white shirt that someone—presumably he himself—had expertly ironed. He looked so much like a butler straight out of Bertie Wooster's circle that I expected him to speak with an English accent, but his voice was pure Dorchester, Massachusetts.

"Adam's in the study," he said, inclining his head to the left beyond one of the sets of double doors off the foyer. That message delivered, he shuffled off in the opposite direction to take up a vacuum cleaner in the center of what appeared to be a warm-up living room of overstuffed sofas and chairs, opening onto a larger living room with still larger sofas and chairs. The furnishings were upscale country and surprisingly feminine, with floral fabrics, needlepoint pillows, and stenciled wood-grained floors. I dimly recalled that Adam and his wife, a semisuccessful TV actress, had been divorced. Had she been responsible for the decor? Or perhaps Adam had purchased the house with all the furnishings intact?

The study had an atmosphere of intense activity. It turned out that Adam had not one assistant but two, both blonde, thin, and pretty, wearing tight jeans and white cotton blouses. They were so generically alike, they might as well have been twins.

Adam was sitting in front of a computer. He was wearing polar-fleece slippers and a full set of pajamas decorated with yellow with blue Scottie dogs. A small bandage bracketed his right eye, the result of his collision with the parakeet cage that had caused such distress the previous morning. Without any greeting, he asked point-blank, "Do you have good taste?"

Since there's no objective answer to that question, I said with a laugh, "Of course!"

"Sit here," he pointed to a chair beside him. "Come look at this wallpaper Web site. The deal is, we've got Mommy coming for Christmas, and she's bringing Sidney Lumet. Already the bitch is throwing out hints that my guest room is too shabby for him! Why can't she book him a room at the Charlotte Inn where *she's* staying? Well, she's tight as a tick, we know that—so I've decided to wallpaper the guest room with something really expensive so I can throw that in her face if I need to."

He tilted his head in my direction as he spoke, but kept his fabulous turquoise eyes shut tight. All people close their eyes for a moment now and then, but I'd never before seen anyone speak as if he were summoning his conversation from the depths of a trance.

All of a sudden I was knee-deep in wallpaper print-outs. "Look at these!" he commanded as his inkjet printer spewed out page after page of variations on one design: a pale pink background with pink, grey, and mauve beaded cameos of Victorian belles. (Clearly, Adam *was* responsible for the home's decor.) "I just can't make heads or tails of these!" he cried in exasperation. "I've talked for *hours* with this sweetheart of a woman, Cynthia, but these are all so much alike, I can't choose one! I just can't!"

I could easily believe that he had spent hours on the phone with Cynthia, though I wondered why a wallpaper company would risk frustrating their nuttier, more compulsive clientele, as typified by Adam Thomas, by providing so many nearly identical choices. I said soothingly, "They're all so similar, and all really pretty; I don't see how you can go wrong with any of them. Just pick one!"

He didn't hear me. Eyes wide open and locked on his computer screen now, he kept the pages churning from the printer, some of them nothing but spec sheets with shipping prices, dimensions, and other hieroglyphics.

Soon I held thirty or more sheets of paper in my lap. Adam said to one of the blonde assistants, his eyes again closed to facilitate speech, "Could you put these in order?"

With a happy smile, the girl took the pages from me, sorted them, and stapled them into separate bundles. She was clearly entranced at the thought of working for the son of two rich and famous people. I wondered—a bit evilly—how long she would continue to perform all sorts of meaningless tasks without a paycheck.

Meanwhile, as more wallpaper samples spilled out of the printer, I thought of the sign I'd taped to the door of my bookshop: *Opening at 1:30 today.* Certainly this was a slow time of the year for island retailers, but I had set aside this hour to consult with this man about parapsychology, not to rack my brain about minor variations in reproduction Victorian wallpaper designs.

"Adam," I said with a sigh, "Can I have a few minutes with you to talk about your ghosts?"

"Oh that," he said with a dismissive wave, eyes glued to the screen. "George can tell you all about it."

"He's—?"

"George!" hollered Adam.

Across two sets of doors opening onto the foyer, the sound of vacuuming ceased. A few moments later, the diminutive, golden-haired "butler" appeared. Adam said, "Tell her about the spirits, will you, George? And show her the room."

As I followed George into the foyer, the front door opened and a black-haired woman in a stylish brown suede jacket poked her head inside. I recognized her as a long-time island caterer, and we greeted one another cheerfully.

George canted his head toward the study and told her in a conspiratorial whisper, "He's got a check for you."

The woman smiled wanly. "It's only been three years."

As George and I mounted two sets of stairs, he filled me in on the home's dark side. He and Adam often heard footsteps coming from the third-floor master bedroom when they knew for a certainty no one else was in the house. They often found objects missing, only to have them turn up a week later in one of the many obvious places where they'd already looked countless times.

On one occasion, the disappearance had turned mean. A pearl necklace that belonged to Adam's daughter vanished from the drawer beside her bed while she was on a visit home from Bard College. Adam accused another young woman who was working for him at the time. The police were summoned, and the girl was both questioned and fingerprinted, after which the disgraced hireling was banished from the house.

The pearl necklace showed up the next day under Adam's pillow.

George said Adam's main concern was that the ghosts were spreading gloom and doom throughout the house. While Adam had never been Mr. Mental Health, he had never before felt so chronically depressed, irritable, and accident prone.

"He and I are constantly tripping. We can't get rid of the feeling we're being pushed. Some of Adam's guests have sensed that their lives were in danger when they stood at the top of the stairs. And the worst part of it all is that Adam has been attracting *bad people!* They think he's got tons of money, and they bilk him for it!"

I stopped and looked at George, who seemed genuinely fond of his employer. I found it telling that whatever malicious entity gathered strength inside these walls, it hadn't been able to infect this good man, other than to cause him obvious sorrow and concern. Possibly his mission to protect Adam served as a true amulet.

"Bad people, huh?" I echoed.

He nodded somberly. I wanted to observe that personalities like Adam's—helpless, entitled, self-centered, oblivious, willing to buy expensive wallpaper while neglecting to pay a caterer for a job performed three years ago—are bound to irritate other people to the point that they might *appear* "bad" (i.e., grasping, carping, and angry). There was a good chance that Adam himself was at the root of these problems.

Or was the house making him that way?

At the third-floor landing we entered through a wide lintel to a room that ran the length and width of the house. Dormered windows faced in every direction, with a central bank of floor-length windows framing the sea. Most Katama architecture goes through comical contortions to catch a peek of the water; this third-floor bedroom positively captured the view.

Ornate antiques were placed around the otherwise modern room, dominated by an elderly mahogany bed burnished black with time. Its scalloped headboard was imprinted with a fading chain of primroses.

Lovely as the room was, I felt an immediate, overwhelming aversion to being there. I felt myself struggling to breathe as I moved through this space suffused with melancholy as thick as Jell-O. Even the spectacular sea view left me unmoved, in fact the lack of pleasure in the view turned my mood even more dismal.

"There's something here," I told George. "Something serious."

Almost arguing with me, he said, "But how could there be ghosts here? Or poltergeists? Or whatever? This house is only seven years old! The man who built it was a periodontist, for crying out loud, with a wife and two little kids! From Ohio! Have you ever heard of anyone or *anything* unwholesome coming out of Ohio?"

Normally I would have laughed out loud at such a comment, but I was feeling increasingly bleak. "Maybe it was brought in with the furniture. Maybe it's the bed."

When we clomped back down the two flights of stairs and reentered the study, I saw something that, in hindsight, struck me as humorous. The caterer was seated in what I'd come to think of as "the hostage chair" in front of the printer, and now *she* held a pile of freshly printed wallpaper pages. Assistant Number One stood at the ready with a stapler.

Adam looked up at me, eyes open. "What do you think?"

How could I tell him that he and his home were a perfect example of negative energy feeding off a vulnerable human, until the two blended together into a white-hot compost, a human and nonhuman *folie à deux?*

George said, "She thinks it could be the bed."

Adam closed his eyes and shuddered. "It's not the bed."

Assistant Number Two called to Adam from the adjoining pantry with a cordless phone in her hand. "Another wallpaper guy is calling with a quote."

Eyes still closed, Adam said, "Not now. . . It's not the bed."

I shrugged. "Well . . ."

Eyes still bulging through thin, pale lids, Adam asked a question in my general direction, "What do you think I should do? Should I move? Can we get an exorcist in here? Will it cost a bundle? Can you do it? Are you going to charge me for it?"

Suddenly I had a good idea of what Adam Thomas should undertake. It wouldn't be easy for him. It might not even be possible, given his deteriorated mental condition. But the healing I had in mind was, I was convinced, his only hope.

One thing I refused to do was to discuss this or any other matter in this zoo of bewildered people led by a man who was deaf to any kind of reason or observation.

I said, "Come see me in my bookstore when you're not so busy. We'll have coffee or hot chocolate, and I'll share my ideas with you. No charge."

At my back as I marched to the front door, I heard him say, "It's not the bed."

———

As of this writing, in early 2008, Adam Thomas has not appeared in my bookstore. But here's the Nadler Remedy, which should more justifiably be called the Aristophanes or the *Commedia del Arte* or the Norman Cousens or Mel Brooks remedy. You've got it—this afflicted man in Katama would need to learn to laugh, a lot, to effect a change in himself and his household.

We know that someone like that is too far gone, too punctured by his own neuroses (or even psychoses), for anything to relieve him truly—not psychotherapy nor psychotropic drugs nor a change of lifestyle, short of holing up in a monastery. But laughter—the kind that originates in the belly and blasts out the chest before erupting vocally—that works as well as anything. It's God's great gift to us. And I could tell that eons had passed since Adam Thomas had found anything even remotely funny.

I would recommend that he devote the next chunk of his life to laughing. He would really need to work at it, but I honestly think that after an hour of guffaws, this morose man would feel a change.

And the bonus is that nasty ghosts don't like laughter.

They don't get it. It annoys them, and, quite speedily, they leave. Or else they too learn to laugh and are cured of their own dark tendencies.

I was reminded of an interview I had with Candace Duark* of Chilmark for a chapter in *Haunted Island*. She'd told me about an experience she had, back in the 1970s, in an old hunting lodge in Vermont. She and her friends who shared the house all had a sense, whenever they bent their heads to a task, of a man standing over them with an ax held high, ready to strike. She found out that the lodge had once been owned by a lumberjack who'd killed his wife and children. A psychic told Candace and her group to cure the phantom of his guilt and dementia by making him laugh. For weeks they told jokes, held wine-tasting revelries, acted goofy, and told more jokes until they were rolling on the floor. "We made him laugh," said Candace, "And then one day his presence vanished from the cottage."

So there you have it—the ultimate exorcism: Throw out the holy water, don't bother to call a priest, just laugh out loud!

LITTLE
GIRL
LOST

I heard a man's voice over the phone asking if I was the woman who conducted ghost research on the Vineyard. It made me sound as if I went about in a white lab coat, pouring beakers of ectoplasm into petri dishes, but I answered in the affirmative.

He sighed. A long pause ensued. I thought he might hang up.

Finally he said, "I never believed in ghosts before. I never believed in *anything* other than the power of science to explain *everything*. But now . . ." Another sigh. Another pause. "My wife and I and our two children have just come back from a Vineyard vacation in a house so . . . so *possessed*, that it's going to be a long while before we rent a place on the island again."

Michael,* a businessman from Coventry, Rhode Island, in his early thirties, proceeded to tell me the following story.

Michael, his wife, Gayle,* and their eight-year-old daughter and five-year-old son rented a four-bedroom cottage for two weeks in July 2004. The 125-year-old Victorian sat on Tuckernuck Avenue, one of the countless streets in Oak Bluffs lined with nineteenth-century houses.

The cottage they stayed in had been purchased a couple of years before by three New York firemen looking for a good investment. One of the new owners told Michael over the phone, "The place was a shambles. You could sit in the living room and see cracks of daylight coming through the walls. They call those old cottages 'Victorian gems,' but if they're allowed to sit and fester, they turn into Victorian mushrooms."

The firemen hired a local contractor, but had also come to the island themselves on weekends to work on the project. "I've wondered ever since if anything weird happened to the firemen," Michael speculated as he told me about his family's stay in the house. "I mean, did they already know the cottage was straight out of *The Rocky Horror Picture Show*?"

The Rhode Island couple found the cottage adorable at first glance. The sloping roof lines, upstairs dormers, and old-fashioned layout (including "railroad" bedrooms upstairs, where one room opens directly into the next) had been preserved, but fresh beaded-pine paneling covered the inside walls, and new beige shingles covered the exterior walls. New windows (in a traditional style), and freshly painted cedar trim provided a clean and snappy look.

"The kids spent the first hour racing up and down the stairs," Michael recalled. "In a downstairs closet they discovered a box of antique children's toys—you know, a toy horse, a couple of old dolls, pick-up sticks, carved wooden cowboys and Indians. We figured the toys had come with the house, because the firemen didn't seem to be into antiques—the furnishings are modern and basic. The kids played with that stuff like they'd never been given a Nintendo DS."

The first night the family strolled into town for pizza at Giordano's, then ice cream down on the docks, followed by a ride on the Flying Horses (the oldest operating carousel in the country) to finish a busy day. "We know how to tire our kids out for an early bedtime," quipped Michael.

Half an hour later, the children were bedded down in two small upstairs rooms with a communicating door open between them. Michael and Gayle settled themselves into the living room downstairs and cracked open some books they'd brought to read. Within half an hour, though, they too became drowsy, and tiptoed up the stairs to their bedroom at the front of the house.

Husband and wife drifted off to sleep, only to be awakened a short while later by the sound of children hooting and laughing maniacally and bounding up and down the wooden staircase.

Michael shouted, "GET BACK IN BED!"

The cacophony continued.

The couple, sitting bolt upright, stared at one another in confusion. Their kids had never misbehaved so boisterously before. Michael got out of bed and hollered through the open door. *Crash! bang!* More thuds up the stairs. A series of snide giggles, sounding strangely amplified, rent the air.

Leaning through the bedroom doorway, Michael could glimpse the top of the staircase. There was no sign of even one marauding child. All sounds from the stairwell had ceased. Totally mystified, he made his way across the narrow corridor to the half-closed door of his daughter's room and craned his head around the door. By the soft glow of the night light that his daughter had insisted they leave on, he could see his child sound asleep, her slender arm wrapped around one of the antique dolls they had discovered earlier in the day. Michael drifted through the room just far enough to peek through the connecting doorway into his son's room. The boy, too, lay sleeping.

From the stairwell, the sound of galloping footsteps and whoops of laughter exploded behind him again.

Michael turned and dashed back to the second-floor landing. Once more, all noises ceased as he stared down the narrow staircase leading to the shadows of the foyer.

When he returned to bed, he asked his wife, "Did we bring along some kids we forgot about?"

The cottage on Tuckernuck remained quiet for the rest of the night.

———

The following day, Michael and Gayle occasionally shot one another a searching glance, but mostly they forgot about the events of the previous evening and went about having a fun vacation.

"It was a little like the shock of hearing about a death," Michael said, "The first step is denial. We were in denial that day."

Back at home after many hours at the beach, Michael barbecued chicken on the grill, and Gayle prepared a rice dish and a salad. "We thought slices of watermelon would pass as a real dessert, but after that the kids pleaded for a walk into town to get ice cream."

Gail had brought up a Parcheesi game, and that engrossed the family for the next hour and a half. The long July evening finally succumbed to darkness. Shadows filled the house, but the foursome felt too satisfied and relaxed to get up and switch on the lights.

On the east side of a house, a single thump sounded, as if a drunken giant had come to call, knocked once, then passed out. The family members looked at one another in surprise. Moments later another hard, hollow thump hit the house, this one coming from a wall closer to the street. Only a moment later, another one landed on the west front corner of the house, as if whoever was doing the pounding had jumped the length of the thirty-foot porch in a single bound. Thump after thump completed a circuit of the house. Another round ensued, this one faster.

Michael told his wife and kids to stay seated as he leapt up and flew to the west windows of the dining room in time, he thought, to catch the perpetrator jogging around the bend. A loud whack landed on the left side of the window, then another on the right as he watched, but no visible figure slipped past the glass.

On the final circuit, the poundings whipped around the house with the speed of an automatic weapon firing across wall after wall.

Then all was quiet. That is, until Michael's daughter piped up, "What was that, Daddy?"

After a long cogitating pause, Michael said, "I don't know. Maybe the plumbing system kicked on."

He'd almost convinced himself.

———

To Michael's relief, the insane pounding on the exterior walls never repeated itself, but the sound of children romping up and down the stairs was a nightly feature. His own two kids, mercifully, always slept through the din. It never ceased to jar Michael and Gayle awake, but they'd taken to rolling their pillows over their ears and tucking back into dreamland.

On the second-to-last day of their vacation, Michael called his business partner back in Rhode Island for their daily morning debriefing. Before they hung up, his partner observed, "Something you should know, man. Have you ever noticed my neurotic habit of staring at my cell phone after I've hung up? I always make sure the call's finished, and no more seconds are being charged. Well, every time you and I say 'over and out,' I see that the call is ongoing. Lately I've held the phone to my ear, and I can hear this little girl babbling away. I know it can't be your daughter, because you wouldn't hand your cell to her after a business call. You're just not that big of a goofball."

"What's the girl saying?" asked Michael uneasily.

"I can't tell, but she's yammering away like she's playing with a litter of cocker spaniel puppies."

Michael decided *not* to mention this to Gayle.

———

On the family's last morning in the house, they spent the time tidying up. Gayle made sure the kids put all the antique dolls and toys back in the box and returned it to the downstairs closet. Finally, with the car packed up and ready to go, the children buckled into the back seat, Gayle riding shotgun, Michael decided they needed a memento snapshot of the house. He dug his camera out of his rucksack and squeezed off a photograph of the cottage in late-morning light.

When the prints came back from his local camera store the following week, Michael gave a start when he came to the photo of his rental house. Perfectly centered in the front parlor window was the image of a little girl, staring out as if wondering where her companions were going—and why they weren't taking her with them.

Shipwreck

I'm often asked whether objects can be impregnated with ghostly material. This question arose, for instance, when an antiques dealer in Edgartown learned she'd acquired a cabinet from a house that she later heard is home to a gaggle of ghosts. Could the haunting carry over to the piece of furniture? she asked me. My answer was hardly reassuring: Possibly—she or whoever purchased it would need to wait and see.

"How would we know?"

"Well, unless you slept overnight in the store, you'd have a hard time knowing. Usually what happens is that someone takes the item home and discovers his or her nights are no longer restful."

"How so?" she asked in a quavery voice.

"Most commonly you'll get thumps and bumps on the walls as if someone's bouncing a ball. You might find windows standing wide open that you know you closed and locked the night before. You might hear a disembodied voice sobbing or sighing as if searching for a lost item, things like that."

"Oh, God!" she groaned. "Should I tell a prospective buyer?"

"That's an ethical question," I said, having experienced the same dilemma back in the '90s when I negotiated vacation rentals and knew in advance—thanks to my ghost research—which houses had skeletons in the closet, so to speak. "Why don't you first see how the cabinet does in the shop? When you open up in the morning, check to see if things are moved around. Any china smashed? Framed pictures removed from hooks and placed, picture-side facing down, on the floor or leaning against the base of the wall?"

The subject reminded me of a valuable piece of flotsam taken from the wreck of a 275-foot luxury steamer, the *City of Columbus*, after it smashed up on Devil's Bridge off the cliffs of Aquinnah on January 18, 1884.

All shipwrecks are tragic, inevitable (in that the sea will always rise up and take its toll), and vicariously thrilling and frightening to every single one of us. The wreck of the *City of Columbus* was just a little bit more so. To read about the Vineyard's most notorious shipping disaster is to feel your chest compress with silent weeping.

———

On a clear night with a chill northwesterly wind, the vessel left Boston with forty-five crewmen and eighty-seven passengers aboard, headed for the warmer climes of Savannah and points still farther south. Captain E. E. Wright had piloted this ship and others countless times through the most treacherous part of western Vineyard Sound. His course should have taken him through that difficult passage, with Tarpaulin Cove to starboard and the Gay Head cliffs to port. Extending out from the cliffs is a one-square-mile stretch of underwater boulders known as Devil's Bridge, and that is where the *City of Columbus* came to grief.

Even scrupulous investigation failed to explain why the vessel veered so devastatingly off course, but the key factors were these: Captain Wright dozed off in the pilot house with the windows closed; the quartermaster at the wheel was experienced but unlicensed; the second mate, delegated to carry out the captain's orders—*"When Tarpaulin Cove bears north, go west-southwest"*—either forgot to pass along the coordinates, or the quartermaster spaced out upon delivery.

As the vessel took its first horrendous hit against one of the unseen boulders, Captain Wright was jolted awake. Springing from the pilot house, he ordered a reverse-thrust maneuver, which only served to wedge the ship more soundly into the rocks. Water gushed aboard. Immense waves battered the hull. The boat listed, and anyone who could—all of them men—shimmied up the ratlines and into the rigging to hang themselves out to freeze while they waited for help.

No attempt was made to save women and children, and all of them perished. Within twenty-four hours of sailing, seventy-five passengers and twenty-eight crewmen were dead.

At daybreak, residents of Gay Head observed the wrecked ship on Devil's Bridge, and many brave lads set out in lifeboats to rescue the handful of survivors clinging to the masts.

First let it be said that, in the wake of any maritime disaster on these shores, Vineyard men have never hesitated to jump into the flimsiest boat and haul off to rescue any survivors. Scores of hardy island men have received medals and other honors for their valor and fearlessness.

But after the bodies were counted, there was always a second reason why islanders were so quick to respond to a wreck: Lots of great stuff would wash ashore! There's an old adage in Aquinnah (formerly Gay Head) that, at first light, all eyes turn to the western shoreline, for this is where all the booty floating in from the vast Atlantic is bound to tumble in with the tide.

City of Columbus, with its plush cabins, Gilded Age public rooms, and kitchen stocked for affluent diners, sent Gay Headers a wealth of belated Christmas treats: hundreds of tubs of butter (which the tax revenue bureaucrats tried to collect), upholstered chairs, paintings, dishes, clothes, jewelry, silverware, even quarterboards with the ship's name embossed, one of which is housed today in the maritime museum at Mystic, Connecticut.

George A. Hough, Jr., author of *Disaster on Devil's Bridge* (Marine Historical Association, 1963), wrote about his family's summer neighbor, Mr. Rogers, who owned a humble cabin on the north shore of the Vineyard: "Over the doorway to the seldom used parlor was an oval tablet of porcelain. It was fancily lettered in faded rose and black: *Social Hall*. Turned out, Mr. Rogers himself had pried it from the wreck of *City of Columbus*, right after it was tossed up on the beach."

We can only imagine how many up-island homes still house a relic or two from that catastrophic night. Did all these pieces carry a psychic imprint of that fateful event? A remnant of the despair felt by a frozen sailor as he hung in the rigging as intervals of blackness, then stark light each time the beam from the Gay Head lighthouse trapped him in its glare? An echo of the screams from the panic-stricken woman whose dress was caught in a heavy metal door below decks? Of the horrified young mother found dead with her lost baby's booties ice-soldered to her skirt?

I would hazard a guess that almost all the islanders who can point to a piece of bric-a-brac and say, "This if from the wreck of the *City of Columbus*" have also experienced certain problems in their homes.

I know of one person in particular . . .

———

The woman was tall and thin in that lanky, rangy way

that is typical of so many Yankee women, thanks to their gene pool and to years of outdoor exercise—tennis, bicycling, and swimming, in this woman's case. She was roughly sixty-five years of age and had inherited a quaint Chilmark homestead with views of Stonewall Beach and Menemsha Pond. I met her at an art opening at the Red Barn gallery. In those days, back in the early '80s, the gallery was owned by a delightful pair of art dealers and antiquarians named Bruce and Brandy.

When our conversation worked around to the subject of hauntings, she told me, "My farmhouse has always been full of creaks and ghosties that go bump in the night, but it's gotten worse lately. And I think this condition of 'worse' started when I moved a particular chair from the dining room to the sunroom. I needed to air out the chair. The truth of the matter is, it had begun to stink!"

The offending piece of furniture was a red-plush upholstered parlor chair from the *City of Columbus*. "My father bought it for forty dollars from a Gay Head native who had four of the darn things and wanted to furnish his house in Danish modern," she explained. "We used to say Dad should have bought the whole set while he had the chance, but now I'm not so sure."

"What's the smell like?" I asked.

"Oh, just an old chair smell—mildew, rot. Frankly, it looks like hell, but I do realize it's a museum piece, so I've resisted having it refinished or reupholstered."

But it wasn't the chair's gamey odor that bothered her most. It was its effect on the cottage itself.

"The first night after I parked the chair out in the sunroom, I went to sleep on that balmy July evening and woke up in February—it was *that* cold! Sure, the window was open, but I'd left it that way to catch a fresh nighttime breeze. I sat up in bed, and I saw a line of white mist waft through the room. It was like an indoor cloud. Eventually it moved through the door into the hallway, and it took the cold with it.

"I thought it was some freak of nature, but the next night the exact same thing happened again! On the third night, the freezing cloud again entered the room, but now a noise came with it! I don't know how else to describe it except to say that it reminded me of a ceramic bowl, filled with silverware, being jostled on top of a tumbling clothes dryer."

"Anything else?" I asked.

"No, but the cloud and the rattling noise have been going on for seven nights now! Seven nights!" she repeated with a shake of the head.

"Have you considered putting the chair back in the dining room?"

She wrinkled the nose in her ultra-tanned face. "The smell makes me queasy. I think I'll see if the historical society will take it. They'll know what to do about its . . . ah, problems . . . won't they?"

———

I've tried asking discreetly whether anyone at the Martha's Vineyard Historical Society, located on School Street in Edgartown, knows anything about a chair that would have been donated to their museum some twenty-five years ago. One historical society executive told me with a sigh, "We have a lot of stuff in storage—God knows what-all." (I was also interested in a grand piano—the first ever shipped to the island, circa 1850. Apparently it was bequeathed to the museum upon the death of Desire Coffin Osborne, whose house stood on North Water Street. I wrote about the captain's wife, the piano, and the ghost in *Haunted Island*.)

It's been almost a century and a quarter since the *City of Columbus* broke up on Devil's Bridge. Presumably, a number of Vineyard homes still house a treasure or two from the wreck. It's also likely that some of the current owners have no idea about the provenance of their peculiar old bit of plunder. A red-plush upholstered parlor chair? (Dozens of them must have washed ashore.) A mahogany cabinet? An ornate gold-leaf frame from a mirror? If you possess such an article, and if your house goes a bit wonky on nights when a northeasterly wind is blowing and the surf is thundering against the western shore, it might be time to make your own tax-deductible donation to the Martha's Vineyard Historical Society.

PORTRAIT OF STEVE

W̶e were both oddballs in ways that folded us—like pancake mix and water—into the batter of kindred spirits. Steve Ellis first came into my bookstore in November 2005. He noticed that I stocked Nathaniel Hawthorne titles, and we were off and running in the first of many long conversations. Steve appropriated Hawthorne, having grown up in Haverhill, Massachusetts, close to the author's old stomping grounds. I too had taken Nathaniel to my heart. As a nineteenth-century Vineyarder, the author had spent time in Edgartown, where he had an affair with a passionate young woman who bore him an out-of-wedlock daughter. He had wanted to marry the girl, but her parents rejected young Hawthorne. The baby died. Not too long ago researchers dis-

covered, in the Edgartown cemetery, a small coffin with remains buried alongside Hawthorne's long-ago sweetheart—
très romantique! Mother and daughter may have formed the
template for the characters of Hester Prynne and daughter
Pearl in *The Scarlet Letter.*

I won't recount in detail any one conversation in which
Steve and I indulged because I'd be obliged to set aside another
full book to do it justice. But suffice it to say, we both loved
to split hairs about areas of mutual interest that would have
made most people squirm.

On a rainy afternoon, after I'd made a cup of hot chocolate for each of us and we had eased into opposite ends of the
bookstore sofa, we might turn our noggins to a list of Henry
VIII's six wives or the first emperors of ancient Rome: "Of
course it was Augustus, then Tiberius . . ." "Did Caligula come
next, or was it Claudius?"

We both loved Rome, in fact, and had spent months at
a time there. Steve, it turned out, had spent part of his Roman
time living *inside* the Vatican. He was some sort of exclaustrated
cleric. (He taught me that word. *Exclaustrated* means living outside a religious order but still affiliated with it; in other words,
freedom without dishonor. This worked perfectly for me, an un-
official nun in the secular world—the kind who lives in her own
apartment and can wear whatever she likes, within reason.)

Steve and I were the same age—we were both born in
1948—but he seemed like a much older person. He was tall
and rotund, with a silver beard and an aristocratic bearing,
and he wore tailored slacks with crisp creases, Englishy pull-
over sweaters, and scarves. He reminded me of an African-
American Orson Wells, and, in truth, he was just slightly on
the pompous side. A heart condition that he was disinclined
to discuss caused him to walk with a cane. In fact, he hardly
seemed to mind stepping into the shoes of an elderly man. He
enjoyed the lunch and the company at the Oak Bluffs Coun-
cil on Aging. After that he would buy a little something from

the antiques store on Tuckernuck Avenue. The last part of this routine was invariably a visit to my bookstore.

Whenever he went missing for a week or two at a time, it seemed to relate to a stay with his father in Haverhill. His mother was somehow absent from the picture, and only when I read his obituary did I learn that he had once been married. He had no children but was fond of his nephews, and he'd inherited a lovely old house from an aunt in Vineyard Haven. (He'd shown me pictures of it only because a huge flock of wild turkeys once invaded his front yard, which sounds quaint until it happens to you.)

Steve once told me one of the eeriest true ghost stories I've ever heard. I'll try to recreate his scholarly, vaguely old-fashioned style as I set it down for you.

I was set to attend a conference in an old monastery, high in the mountains, about an hour's drive from Boulder, Colorado. There was no longer a religious community installed there, so they closed it up every winter, and opened it in the spring for meetings and retreats.

I took down the date of the event, but I got it wrong somehow, and booked my flight a day before anyone else did. I received word back that it was not a problem, that the day staff from the village had been getting the place organized. If I didn't mind spending the first night alone in the monastery, I was welcome to come up early.

This would have been a perfect time for Steve to take a reflective pause. He was a riveting story-teller with a sonorous tenor voice. He reminded me of one of those nineteenth-century narrators who could recount a novella-length story until dawn, and no one at the dinner table would make a sound other than to pour a fresh glass of good port.

I was tired from the flight, and even wearier

from the long, twisting drive through the mountains. Finally, I reached the wrought-iron gates which, thankfully, stood open. The sun was just sinking toward the surrounding mountain peaks, and that last bit of amber light beautifully illuminated the massive stone walls. The stone itself, even without the sunset, was a golden color. It had been brought in from some other mountain range because it was similar in hue to the ancient walls of Jerusalem. The whole place had a Knights Templar feel to it.

When I pulled up through the porte-cochere, two brass lanterns glowed on either side of the high wooden doors. A caretaker came out, showed me where to park, then opened the doors again and led me through the front hall the size of a school auditorium.

The place was awash in gloom. The caretaker had switched on only enough wall sconces for us to make our way up the grand staircase and through a maze of corridors. Finally he showed me into my room—very comfortable, with a four-poster bed, dark mahogany furniture, and some tattered but very noble old Persian carpets. I moved around the room switching on every lamp because, by then, the sun had dropped well below the mountains. No light whatsoever came through the recessed Gothic windows.

The caretaker said he was heading back to his cabin behind the main building. He asked if I remembered the route we'd taken to get to my room, and then he described how to find the dining hall downstairs. "Most of the food supplies won't be brought up until tomorrow, but there's bread, butter, eggs, and a few cans of this and that in the pantry, if you want to help yourself."

I'll admit, immediately after the caretaker had gone, I toyed with the idea of locking myself in my room and not coming out until daylight. Up until that evening, I'd only had the haziest sense of the existence of ghosts, but, alone in that vast, silent place, I couldn't help thinking that all the spirits from a hundred-mile vicinity—dead monks and cowboys and ancient Indians—were massing inside the thick walls for the night.

However, as often happens with me [and here he patted his Orson Wells tummy under the dark sweater], I was finally overcome with hunger pangs, and suddenly nothing else mattered.

Steve described how he'd padded down one corridor after the next, feeling for light switches, sometimes finding them, sometimes not. A couple of times he had to double back, and finally, when he thought he'd lost all sense of direction and would have to sleep in some unknown bedroom—without a single belonging, not even a toothbrush—he rounded a bend and found himself at the top of the grand staircase. From there he could follow the caretaker's directions to the pantry off the dining hall.

In the big—and I have to say, freezing—dining hall, I turned on a couple of table lamps, but I couldn't find a main switch for the chandelier or anything that could really light up the place. I dimly made out a space as big as a ballroom, with a terracotta tiled floor and a collection of rustic tables and old Windsor-backed chairs. Along one wall ran a long row of clerestory windows and on the other side was a tremendous hearth—cold and dark, of course.

Into this complete isolation and silence, certain sounds would intrude: a twig tapping a window, a pipe gurgling, a thump from something rolling off a bureau in a faraway room. All of it perfectly innocent, and yet momentarily terrifying as it punctuated the quiet, especially with my nerves wound so tight. Each time I let out a little gasp, then chuckled nervously as if—well, as if, were anyone watching me, I was signaling how absurd it was to feel so nervous."

Finally Steve's hunger propelled him across the dining hall and into the dark but comfortably utilitarian kitchen. He located a family-sized can of beef stew and, without having to open too many drawers, excavated a can opener. He sloshed the entire contents into a casserole dish, and while it heated in the microwave, Steve checked inside the big refrigerator. Six or seven bottles of white wine stood on the highest shelf.

I would have preferred red wine with the stew, but I didn't want to waste more time searching for it—can you imagine venturing down into some dungeon of a wine cellar? No thank you! I examined each bottle in the fridge to find which one appeared to be the cheapest. I didn't want to seem greedy by opening up a whole bottle of their best wine just for myself. I had every intention, however, of drinking half of it. I realized I'd need to imbibe some courage for the long trek back to my room.

Steve found a seat in the corner of the dining hall. He'd pulled four or five dingy-beige cloth napkins from a pile. One he'd used as a potholder to transport the hot casserole dish to the table. Another he spread out as a makeshift placemat, and a third he tied around his neck to keep his sweater clean for the weekend. After thirst and hunger were at least partially sated, he began to look around the room.

Now that's odd, I told myself, when my glance roved over the platform below the hearth. I hadn't noticed, when I first came through the room, that a covered statue stood at the far end, some slab of something, protected by a white drop cloth. But then the thing, whatever it was, started to move. In another moment, I realized that it was a figure of a seated monk, and it was slowly revolving toward me.

His robes were white, and I now wondered how they could have ever resembled the rough material of a drop cloth; they were made of some sheeny, soft satin, folds upon folds of cloth, just like those voluminous cloaks we see on saints in seventeenth-century paintings. Very little of his face showed beneath the cowl. What small glimpse of skin I saw— just a bit around his nose and bracketing his mouth— was so pale that I thought he might be an albino.

My questions piled on top of each other: "When did you get here? What order are you from? Why didn't anyone tell me you'd be here too?" And then I realized he was going in and out of focus, with wavy lines, as if he existed on an old strip of celluloid in a movie. I had the impression that none of my questions registered with him, but somehow *I* registered. I could sense him taking me in, considering me as if the world and time itself depended on the conclusion he drew. And you know . . . even though I could hardly see his face, a melting kindness seemed to pour from his eyes. At last he said, in a voice that was no more than a whisper but perfectly distinct, even from a good fifty feet away, "We'll meet once more." Then he seemed to pull his robes tighter around him as if they were blankets, and he disappeared.

By April 2007, Steve Ellis and I had known one another for a little more than two years. We'd never made a plan or anything resembling a date. The affection between us was in no way romantic, although something about our long, involved conversations, and our instant intimacy, made me think we'd once shared a grand passion—though perhaps in an elevated, ecclesiastical kind of way—in earlier lives. Once in the beginning of our friendship, he dropped by the bookstore two days in a row and we had one of those odd epiphanies: I emerged from my office, my mind in a fog, and was taken aback to see him so soon again. In the next instant I could tell that he had read the alarm on my face and felt that he was intruding. He left hurriedly, and after that was careful to space his visits at least two weeks apart.

I felt no rush to alter our pattern, though when a month or two went by without my seeing Steve, I actually ached for him. That's what happens when you're deprived of your truly favorite conversationalist.

The last time I saw Steve, I lent him a CD of music by Hildegard of Bingen, fourteenth-century composer of angelic melodies, and he in return let me borrow an audiotape of his own favorite Gregorian chants. In the second week of May, it occurred to me I hadn't seen Steven in nearly three weeks, and that meant that any moment he would be jaunting through the door. Holding his dapper cane off the floor, he would greet me with something like, "I thought of you the other night when I picked up a book about Eleanor of Aquitaine."

Instead, flipping through the current newspaper, I saw Steve's face on the obituary page. He'd died on May 8 and been discovered dead in bed. A memorial service had already been held for him in Haverhill.

Had the monk in the white robes returned for him?

It was the following November when Steve's ghost began to gently haunt me. Sometimes I think the way to summon a departed spirit is to incorporate the image of that person in your daily rounds. Any discussion of saints, mystics, European history, and "fights historical, from Marathon to Waterloo, in order categorical" brought Steve to the forefront of my thoughts. Tuckernuck Antiques became one of my daily walking destinations. I sometimes purchased items there despite the fact that I'd spent the last few years getting rid of stuff as I moved to smaller and smaller domiciles, and I concluded that I must be under Steve's influence.

And then his influence became more direct. I'd been using my digital camera almost nightly in an effort to pick up ghost anomalies. Nothing out of the ordinary had shown up for many nights running, until one chilly night my steps took me to the triangle of park alongside Tuckernuck Antiques. I realized I hadn't yet taken any photos of this special place, so I held up the camera and said out loud, "Okay, Steve, this is your chance to send me a message."

The camera died. The display flicked to black. I poked and prodded at the power switch and every other button on the little panel. Did the battery need a recharge? Apparently not, for when I got home the camera surged back on.

Next morning at first light, I scurried back to the antiques store, snapping perhaps a dozen shots on my way over. And the camera went on working as I *click-click-click*ed the facade of Tuckernuck Antiques. On my seventh shot, I announced to Steve, "Last chance to send a message." Immediately the camera's screen faded to black. Once again I could not get it restarted.

Steve's presence continued for a couple more weeks. Orbs the size of bubbles appeared in my photos of "his" places. Well into December the four clay pots outside my bookstore still bristled with red geraniums, yellow marigolds, purple pansies, and luxuriant trellises of rosemary. My planters were the only ones that still held live plants into December. Everyone else's had croaked. If it wasn't Steve's spirit effecting this abracadabra, then some other helpful angel had been sent my way.

But the jewel in the crown of Steve's November/December 2007 communication with me happened the night after the camera died outside the antiques store.

I was sitting upstairs in my apartment, and the night had grown quiet enough that I could hear music floating up from the bookstore. For three days straight I'd been playing—on repeat mode, no less—a CD of classical pieces, most of them far too famous and therefore overplayed, such as Beethoven's *Fur Elise* and Debussy's *Clair de Lune*. But I enjoyed the easy listening, and I was still trying to flush the memory of all the seventies disco music my two young employees had played nonstop all through the summer.

Finally, I changed from "touristy classical," to an all-Chopin disc. This too I'd played more times than was good for my mental health, but in its favor, there was only one selection I truly couldn't stand, the too-peppy *Valse Brillante*, which I normally skipped completely.

So when I heard Chopin's melodies tinkling up from the store, I kicked myself for forgetting to click off the CD player, even though it meant dragging out a stepladder, placing it under a high shelf, and climbing up to hit the stop button.

I padded downstairs in my pajamas and slippers, unlocked the rear office door, and let myself into the bookstore. At night I keep a ring of small lamps with floral, opaque glass shades lit to serve as night lights. The bookstore walls are framboise red, and the bookcases are antique or distressed to look reasonably old. In this low-lit, cozy setting, an unexpected track of music greeted me.

It was Tchaikovsky's *Nocturne in F,* the first piece on the first CD of the world's most relaxing classical music. The one I'd been listening to for three days straight, but not on this day, not this evening. Yet here it was; the air was filled with Tchaikovsky's fairy-light, tinkling piano melody.

This was so like a supernatural event that had startled me nearly four decades ago—when a deceased friend changed the record on my phonograph from Scott Joplin to James Taylor—that I identified it and accepted it immediately for the otherworldly hello that it was.

In stark contrast to the long-ago night when an apparent ghost's hand on a phonograph had frightened me from my house, never to return except to collect my belongings, this time I stepped into the room and let Tchaikovsky's chords surround me like a cashmere shawl. During a paranormal event such as this one, you can't point to a particular departed soul with one hundred percent certainty, yet I was convinced this was surely another visit from Steve.

But that wasn't the end of it. As the *Nocturne* played, I drifted over to a cafe table facing the length of the store. I propped my elbows on the table, chin in my hands, and listened to the music, as rapt as if a live pianist performed for me alone.

The music ended. I tried to remember what came next on deck. Was it Bach? Pachelbel? A long silence ensued, longer, I thought, than the normal interval between tracks. And then a new piece of music struck up with its own signature frenzy. It was the *Valse Brillante.* From the Chopin CD.

I burst out laughing, dragged over the stepladder, and shut down the music for the night.

The haunting tapered off after that. It will be interesting to see if Steve has paid his regards in full and made his way to the next part of his journey—a journey that doesn't include me, at least not for now. But I really won't mind if I continue to have this interesting figure as my good ghost friend.

Random Ghosts II

A ccidents like this shouldn't happen. That is, we decline to waste time worrying that this particular misfortune will befall us. We worry about such things as slipping in the tub, or having a truck plow into us, or getting electrocuted while prying a mangled bagel from the toaster.

We have no concerns, however, about being struck by lightning indoors with all the windows closed.

In December 1851, Mrs. Elwina Norris, a whaling captain's widow, invited some lady friends for afternoon tea at her home at the corner of Main and Spring streets in Vineyard Haven—the corner where Mardell's card and gift store has stood for decades.

It was a cloudy day, but not even a drizzle had dampened the ground when Mrs. Norris's friends gathered in the front parlor around the festive table strewn with teapot and padded cozy, dainty bone china cups, pongee-silk napkins, and a three-tiered platter of cookies and little sandwiches.

A fire blazed and crackled in the hearth. When it showed signs of burning low, Mrs. Norris tinkled a bell and her new "girl," a month off the boat from Ireland, appeared to feed a fresh chunk of wood to the coals. Conversation centered on gossip and town doings. If anything critical had happened anywhere else in the world—or even across Vineyard Sound—no one spoke of it or even knew about it.

In the distance, far beyond the lace-curtained windows facing the harbor, an occasional boom of thunder made itself known. The women paused, teacups halfway to their lips, pinky fingers extended as they'd seen in the pages of *Ladies' Home Journal,* and then the chatter started anew.

Presently, strong winds rattled the shutters and shook the house. The afternoon grew preternaturally dark. Mrs. Norris assured the ladies they were welcome to shelter in the house as long as they needed to. "The girl can always fix up beds for you. And we have a lamb roast planned for this evening."

The tea-party guests nodded and chuckled. This sleepover sounded more amusing than returning to their homes, with all the attendant obligations. As they entertained this notion, a fireworks display of lightning flared in the northeast-facing windows. And as always happens when lightning strikes so close, a Vulcan-sized burst of thunder slammed into the house, shaking the floors and the ladies' chairs. Shrieks and nervous laughter followed.

"Thank goodness lightning never strikes twice," said Mrs. Norris. "And that, my dears, is scientific fact."

Famous last words.

In the next moment, the flames in the fireplace were drawn upward in a shower of sparks, as if the chimney were inhaling. Then, instantaneous with a cannonball of thunder, a rush of static propelled itself out of the fireplace. The guests watched in horror and amazement as a spear of lighting, bright as molten yellow-white lava, shot out of the chimney, struck Mrs. Norris in the ear, then fired up through the top of her head in a geyser of sparks, the trajectory of the lightning shaped like a check mark through the woman's head. Her tea cup and plate clattered to the floor.

She died seated in her chair. Her neck was scorched, but her face was untouched.

Coincidentally, at what was reckoned to be the very same moment—or close to it—diagonally across the street, in a stable that has long been the site of a shop called Bowl 'n Board, a painter named Francis Nye, Jr., was also struck by lightning and killed on the spot. This strangely homicidal pair of lightning bolts still has meteorologists scratching their heads. Lightning bolts are often branched, so it could have been a single event. Still, it was very odd that one bolt would kill two victims separated by a distance of fifty yards.

Historians chalk up this story to the ferocity of storms in earlier days. No modern-day squalls come close to that afternoon tempest of a century and a half ago, despite hints that global warming may already be leading to stronger storm systems. Meteorological trends notwithstanding, those of us whose eyes widen at any hint of the supernatural have to ask ourselves whether that storm of 1851 had fantastical dimensions, particularly after perusing the *Vineyard Gazette*'s description of the horror: "The cloud from which the electrical fluid was discharged, hung directly over Holmes Hole for twenty or thirty minutes, during which time there was an almost uninterrupted flash of lightning and roar of thunder. The scene was frightful and appalling, and made the stoutest hearts to quail."

Could it happen again?

The widow Norris said it could not.

I rest my case.

———

A couple of weeks into my ghost-walk tours of 2007, I bought a new lantern. Kerosene lanterns had been part of my *schtick* since I started the nighttime walks in 1993. They last a long time, shed a beautiful light, and put us in mind of ghost-hunters (and ghost victims) past. Also in the lanterns' favor, they haven't once caught my skirt on fire, an eventuality that people who know me and my Calamity Jane tendencies will swear is bound to happen.

The new lantern was larger than the ones that had come before it—about the size of a twelve-cup coffeemaker. The first night I used it on my Vineyard Haven tour, I found the wick needed constant adjustment. Sometimes the flame flared too high; other times it diminished to the point of going out. I did not blame this on any paranormal activity. The lantern was obviously a faulty product that would need to be replaced.

At one point in my Vineyard Haven walk I have the group pause outside the oldest house—quite plain and in need of a fresh paint job—on a rutted dirt road known as Cromwell Avenue. Due to its choice location near the harbor, this lane was once the thriving commercial strip of old Holmes Hole. Imagine a town out of *Pirates of the Caribbean*, with taverns, ships' chandleries, sailors with cards in hand draped around barrels, and horses and wagons trundling past at all hours of the day and night.

Nowadays, the only shop overlooking the unpaved Cromwell Lane is the oh-so-tasteful and expensive Midnight Farm, a housewares and apparel shop co-owned by Carly Simon. The rest of the dusty half-block is quiet and dark. The scariest sight a stroller would be likely to encounter is the occasional skunk rooting in someone's trash bin—though one evening that same summer we were startled to see a naked man in the window of his apartment over Ripley's Reads, a children's bookstore terraced high above Cromwell Avenue. He gazed out at the twenty or so people in my ghost walk group, then slowly pulled his drapes closed.

It was at this spot (though not on the Naked Man Night) that someone asked me whether I believe in demonic possession. If I'd had a chance to answer, I would have said, hedging my bets, "I do, but in my opinion the phenomenon is rare." My response was cut off, however, because at that exact instant a fireball erupted in my new lantern. It looked for a moment as if it might shatter the glass. I almost dropped the lantern. Instead, my instinct for thrift took over (I'd just shelled out twenty bucks for the contraption, after all) and I spun the wick control all the way down. The fireball vanished, leaving black smudges on the glass.

Then it was impossible to relight the lantern. I tried it with other people cradling it. I held it while other people flicked their lighters. Those able men who love rescue remedies took a turn with it. The wick refused to let a single flame be coaxed from it.

We finished the walk in darkness, a particularly stressful circumstance during our final tramp through the ancient cemetery situated in the heart of town. Leading the way, I tread carefully in the dark, but I took a header over one of those foot-high gravestones. I'd like to say a ghost pushed me, but I knew this was more of an example of the *I Love Lucy* factor in my life.

For the Edgartown tour a few days later, I managed to relight the lantern. Once again, the wick required constant fiddling. And another fireball was in the offing.

You'll recall that the first fireball occurred as the key words *demonic possession* were uttered. The second was activated when I stood on the steps of the Federated Church on South Summer Street and described a minister who preached hellfire and brimstone sermons. Yes, it was on *hellfire and brimstone* that the lantern got jiggy again. This time, it happened earlier in the tour (about 8:15), so enough light remained for all of us to see a cloud of black smoke billowing out through the perforated metal top.

"I'm going to bury this haunted lantern at the crossroads at midnight," I joked nervously.

That turned out to be unnecessary: I returned the lantern to the hardware store and received a new model that worked perfectly for the rest of the summer.

———

"Come on, honey, show her that bizarro picture."

It was the start of my Ghosts of Edgartown walking tour one July day in 2007. I'd just gathered together my group of twenty or so people, among them an outgoing mom and her fifteen-year-old daughter. The girl had a moon-shaped face and a typically sullen adolescent disposition, which kept her forehead furrowed and her mouth puckered. This seemed like a classic mother/teenager outing: daughter had been willing to join mom on a ghost-hunting tour, but their "togetherness" was maintained by the teen keeping a twenty-foot distance.

✗ As we descended the wooden steps of Edgartown Books, the mother prompted again over the bobbing heads, "Sweetie, show the lady your picture! She'll love it!"

The girl shook her head in vigorous refusal.

And so the hour unfolded as we visited sites of apparent hauntings, including my favorite: the six late-seventeenth-century Mayhew gravestones standing a mere twenty feet back from the sidewalk, surrounded by roses and hydrangeas—just your average Edgartown front yard. The evening softened as antique lamps twinkled on inside the quaint captains' houses. (I've always thought that even without the ghost stories, a

✗ *I bought this book here.*

10/11

stroll through nighttime Edgartown weaves an inexorable spell of enchantment.)

At the end of the walk, when I deposited my guests on the upper terrace of Memorial Wharf overlooking the harbor and the dark shores of Chappy, I noticed that mother and daughter had drawn together.

In a voice that had lost its pushiness (now that she and her child enjoyed a temporary truce), the mother said, "Can you show her your picture now?"

The girl had her cell phone ready for display in her hand. She held up a digital photo a friend had snapped of her an hour and a half earlier as they finished dinner at a cafe called The Newes of America, operating in the Kelley Hotel right in the heart of town. The hotel has long been said to be haunted—something about a man hanging himself on the third floor and a spectral lady who materializes in the laundry room. The management of the cafe, a brick enclave in the oldest part of the building, is so aware of the hotel's reputation for ghosts that it runs an article about them on its menu: "Would you like a ghoul's appearance along with that quesadilla?"

The sullen teen's face filled the screen, and she hadn't bothered to dignify the picture with even a wan smile. I recognized the ancient brick wall behind her that gives The Newes its charm, but what I didn't—couldn't—recognize was the powdery white face peering over the subject's shoulder.

Every so often I'll encounter some element of the supernatural that seems more Hollywood than "real" (if the skeptics among you will allow me to use that term). When children on my walking tours ask me if my ghost stories are scary, I try to make the distinction between a skeleton wielding a scimitar in a movie and the different but equally frightening image of a figure looming in an upstairs window when you know for a fact no one is home.

This face in the girl's cell phone photo was of the Hollywood variety while, at the same time being absolutely, or so it appeared, real. The features bore that mummified look of layers of half-decomposed wrappings. The eyes were small, dark, and without life or soul. The face had no more animation than a mask, but, if this was a mask, it lacked any aesthetic or ornamental value.

I stared a long time at the image, then, handing the camera back to the girl, I said, "I don't know who or what this is, but it's the freakiest thing I've ever seen step into a picture."

She rewarded me at last with a genuine smile.

—

Nothing seems amiss—from a paranormal perspective—about the Union Chapel in Oak Bluffs. This grey-shingled bastion of Sunday worship, concerts, and lectures has stood for nearly a century and a half on a rise just to your left as you clear the long commercial block of Circuit Avenue.

The Union Chapel is so much a part of our summer cultural scene that we often take it for granted. But if you stand back and train a fresh eye on the structure, you end up renewing your sense of awe at its grandeur and originality.

A major architect of the nineteenth century, S. F. Pratt, who seemed to take much of his inspiration from sixteenth-century Parisian buildings, Loire Valley chateaux, and, closer to home, Newport mansions, designed the Union Chapel with almost reckless flair. At the tippy-top of the already interestingly shaped octagonal building, a six-sided crown of triangular dormers, dominated by a cone-shaped ninety-six-foot spire, gives the look of an origami construction made solid. And as if one sky-piercing spire were not enough, Pratt added an ornate bell tower, thrusting up alongside the western doors. This tower, unhappily, sheered off and smashed to pieces during the Big Blow of 1933.

At the chapel's ground-floor level, four vaulted double-door entrances face out in each compass direction. The original shingles of the roofline were banded with cream and burgundy stripes, the intricate motif repeated on the long-lost bell tower.

Oak Bluffs (formerly Cottage City) is still recovering architecturally from the blowback of most of the twentieth century, when arbiters of taste decreed that Victorian design was as silly as beribboned poodles. That was the time of the dismantling of towers, bay windows, gingerbread trim, and every other species of "frippery." If these design Nazis could have run completely amok (and they very nearly did), they would have flattened the sloping rooflines, dormers, gables, and verandas of every house built from the 1860s to the 1890s.

During the last four decades, devotees of Victorian design have been putting it all back. Perhaps one day the Union Chapel will be completely reconstituted, up to and including the cream and burgundy stripes and the bell tower.

The fancy-pants church went up in 1871. A little-known fact at that time—or at this time, for that matter—was that the project was sponsored not by a pious church group but by the area's most aggressive developer, the Oak Bluffs Land and Wharf Company.

The investors urgently needed to prove to the denizens of the Methodist Campground that the secular developments springing up on every side of their sacred site were intended for *churchgoing* homeowners. It's difficult to grasp today how the Campground Association could have seemed so intimidating, but clearly that group of tough businessmen felt their livelihood depended on raising, of all things, a church.

Yes, the Methodists were concerned that they were outnumbered by the heathens. In response to the depraved town springing up all around them (well, there *were* illegal saloons, noisy amusements such as a dance hall and a skating rink, and even a house of ill repute), the camp meeting folks erected a seven-foot fence clear around their twenty acres. They even threatened to move lock, stock, and Bible to another parcel of land they had purchased in East Chop. If that failed to protect them from the stain of secularism, they planned to pack up lock, stock, Bible, *and cottage*, and decamp to a wilderness area in Maine.

This would have dealt hurtful PR to the investors ("DE-VELOPERS DRIVE CHURCH GROUP OFF ISLAND"). Bad idea, considering that the Methodists' White City had always constituted the big draw for summer visitors to Cottage City.

But now the developers could point to the Union Chapel and say, "Ta-dah! A house of worship! Christian! We've got it all right here!"

Several years later the developers quietly sold the chapel to a Christian association, and no one was the wiser about its original dollars-and-cents origins. (You won't find this tidbit in any of the old or more recent newspapers, nor in any of our island history books. I came across the info at the *Gazette* archives in a typed letter from Ellen Weiss, author of *City in the Woods* [Oxford University Press, 1987], buried in a pile of clippings about the Union Chapel.)

Which brings us to the haunted nature of this Victorian valentine of a chapel.

As I've always maintained, the untold stories—the stupidly withheld secrets—which are harder to pry loose from the past than coffin lids from perma-sealed caskets, are what cause the negative vortices to flourish in psychic fields.

We know how obsessive-compulsive people are hard to take in the human dimension. Just imagine the same mental disorder in a group of discarnate souls desperate to make a single point: "If someone would just get this story straight, we could pack up and get some Afterlife psychotherapy!" I believe some depraved cleric/enforcer of the long-ago Methodist camp meeting crew is still incensed at the venal genesis of the Union Chapel. Perhaps it's the spirit of the Reverend Hatfield, who organized vigilantes to root out booze from Cottage City hotels. Maybe it's Campground trustee Andrew Dixon White—academic, theologian, and president of Cornell University—who wrote fiery letters to the editor, accusing the town of "blasphemy and eroticism," and became apoplectic when he spied Methodist teens skating to the organ strains of *Nearer My God to Thee*. The religious conflict and paranoia in Cottage City spawned enough fanatics to stock a new round of Salem witch trials. One of those fanatics, in spectral form, appears to hover over the Union Chapel to this day.

How do I know the chapel houses a mad-as-hell minister ghost? Instead of answering directly, I'm going to propose a field trip: Grab your camera and walk around to the east exterior wall of the building. (I always think of it as the dark side.) Snap some pictures of the tall pair of windows on this segment of the octagon. If it's the off-season and the porch lights are extinguished, take pictures of the high double doors facing in the direction of Ocean Park.

If your camera is digital, you can, of course, examine your images immediately. If you use film, you'll need to wait for the photos to be developed. In either case, take a look at the results. You might not even need your glasses.

You see what I mean?

Pilgrim Paranormal Research

DANGER!
OUIJA
ON BOARD

As fascinated as so many of us are by the realm of the supernatural, we can't help but be aware of all the charlatans who've given it a bad rep. One of the more infamous was nineteenth-century Boston photographer William Mumford, who superimposed a hazy portrait of the late Abraham Lincoln standing behind and resting a hand on the shoulder of Mumford's living subject, the widowed Mary Todd

Lincoln. Books on spirit photography still reproduce this picture without any reference to the portrait photographer's trial and conviction in New York for defrauding his clients by dolling up his photo backgrounds with translucent dead people.

Of course, when you're in a rational, pragmatic frame of mind, practically every prop and feature in a ghost hunter's arsenal seems, at first glance, to be extraordinarily silly. Ouija boards are a case in point. To be frightened of this simple bit of equipment—or more accurately, to be respectful of the warning label attached to it—seems farfetched. Still, after a number of years at work in the field, so to speak, you recognize the validity of most of the tools and come to understand the reasons behind the caution labels.

I once thought Ouija boards were as harmless as the other board games with which they're displayed in stores—the Monopoly, Parcheesi, and Clue sets. And every teen growing up in America in the last six or seven decades has acquired a Ouija board somewhere along the line and had a grand old time seeking answers to such weighty matters as "Who will I marry?" and "Am I going to be a millionaire when I grow up?" Not to mention the kids who, senses heightened and hormones raging, attempt to spike their new obsession with the paranormal by pointing a Ouija planchette at it.

My mom's friend Patti Bowen was typical. Back in the 1960s when Patti was a teen, she attended a sleepover at a friend's summer house. The parents were away, thinking the pajama party girls would be safe with nary a bottle of booze or a pack of boys anywhere in the vicinity. It never occurred to them to worry about the Ouija board one of the girls brought with her.

It was a cold night in April, so most of the furniture was still swaddled in old sheets, and the windows and doors facing the lake were boarded up, as they had been all winter. The girls lit the ornate candelabra and set up the Ouija board on the onyx black dining-room table. As two of the girls placed slender white fingers on the planchette, one of the onlookers exclaimed, "Let's call up Jack the Ripper!"

"Good idea!" sang the others.

Clairvoyants worth their salt will shudder at the ignorant audacity of it. They know that even requesting the presence of a benign spirit can invite quite the opposite into the room with you. But as psychologists always point out, teens have no sense of their own mortality and will try anything once.

Patti and her friends applied themselves to the task. In the flickering shadows of the chilly room, all eyes were on the planchette with its complement of fingers. It began to move until it spelled out, "I'm here."

Excitedly the girls debated what to ask first: "Should we ask him his real identity?" "Is he reincarnated?" "Did he kill other women no one ever knew about?"

But before they could agree on a question, a crashing sounded from the kitchen.

The girls were stunned into stillness. Only their eyes moved as, huddled at one end of the table, they ran a head count. All five were present and accounted for.

Another crashing noise erupted, echoing in the dark and rambling cottage.

The girls shrieked. Like a flock of terrified geese, they scooted up the staircase in a flurry of pressed-together bodies. They spent the night locked in the bathroom as noises continued to reverberate from the kitchen. Dishes were tossed and broken again and again, as if the summer kitchen held as much crockery as a restaurant in a grand hotel. Pots and pans banged together. It sounded like a hoarde of demons playing a back beat that was music only to their own pointy ears.

Three of the girls eventually managed to fall asleep, curled into fetal balls on the cold linoleum floor. Patti and one other girl stayed awake all night, sitting back to back and squeezing hands as the sounds of annihilation continued. Not until first light did the hellish din taper off.

Later, in full morning light, the girls tiptoed downstairs to assess the damage. How in the world would they explain to their parents what havoc had been unleashed in this summer kitchen?

When they reached the kitchen doorway they were stopped in their tracks by the sight of clean counters and a spotless floor. Opening the kitchen cabinets, they saw perfectly stacked piles of plates, crocks, and mugs. The carnage from the night before had either been imaginary or impeccably tidied up.

The girls threw jackets over their pajamas and carried the Ouija board down to the edge of the lake, where they dug a four-foot hole in the semifrozen ground and buried the evil toy. It's probably safe to speculate that not a single one of these girls ever participated in a Ouija binge again. However, we have to wonder whether that summer home continued to channel the presence of the last fiend in history we'd ever want running amok in a vacation spot—or anywhere else for that matter.

———

My buddy Bob Alger, of the Pilgrim Paranormal Research group, who has helped me with investigations here on the island, developed a relationship with a Ouija board in his Army days.

"Two other guys and I got hold of a Ouija set, and for several weeks we'd fiddle around with it late at night. For a long time we got nothing, but we persisted, and suddenly someone came through—a Scandinavian fellow named Haln who'd been a merchant in Savannah, Georgia."

Haln told them he'd died when someone had broken into his shop and set fire to it. "He let us know he liked to drink and smoke. We'd place a lit cigarette at the edge of the board and sometimes we'd see the orange end send off sparks as some unseen entity drew on the filter. When we went out, we'd leave a glass of beer beside the board, making a mark where the brew topped off. When we'd get back, we always saw that at least an ounce had been guzzled.

"After that, we got the impression our guest had changed personalities, that either Haln was getting feistier, or he'd been replaced, so we asked one night 'Who is here with us?' The disk spelled out L-I-V-E. One of us had already heard about this handle being used in the spirit world, that spelled backward it was E-V-I-L."

The room got cold and the candle flickered.

"We threw that board out with our empty beer bottles."

———

Some years back, my then husband, Marty, and I had a working relationship with a Ouija board. Marty's a comedy writer—a cute, curly-haired, funny man whom you would never associate with parapsychological abilities—but whenever the two of us sat down with the board, that planchette would dart around like a silver slug in a pinball machine. "Are you doing it?" "No, are you?" we always asked each other, both equally surprised at the energetic results we produced.

Members of the family sometimes wanted us to get in touch with a departed loved one. Once we turned our inquiries to my Great-Grandma Olga. I'd only met her once, when I was four, and she died the following year, but I've always regarded as my leading guardian angel.

"Grandma Olga, have you been reincarnated in any of your descendants?" I asked.

"Patrick" she said, naming the son of my cousin Christopher, who lives in Ireland. Perhaps unconsciously I'd heard this name before and conjured it up from my hidden memories, but consciously I had no idea who "Patrick" was until I later spoke with my mother about it.

After my favorite aunt died, Marty and I received a request from my mother to try to contact her deceased sister via Ouija, just to find out what was what in the Afterlife.

Aunt Meta seemed to come on board—pun intended—just

as requested. All was well with her. She was spending quality time with her late husband, Max, who had died back in the early 70s, and with my father—her brother-in-law—who'd predeceased her by two years. She sounded so happy in the Elysian Fields that I decided to go for the gold and ask a question that would satisfy the theologian in me:

"Meta, on the Other Side, do you feel closer to God?"

The planchette, which had been scooting all over the board, came to an abrupt halt. It was dead in the water. For a full minute we stared at the unmoving wedge of tan plastic. At last I said with a sigh, "I guess there are certain things we're not supposed to be told directly. We have to wait for our own firsthand experience."

We returned to small talk with Meta—Max was fine; my dad was fine; Meta's *bubbe,* who had died in the late 1920s, was fine and dandy—and then we retired the board.

The next morning I discovered that an anomaly had developed with our kitchen door. This was a brand-new house on Trade Winds Road just outside the center of Oak Bluffs, and everything had been working splendidly. Now the kitchen door suddenly refused to close. I examined it closely and determined that the protruding latch that's supposed to retract when it encounters the strike plate was not gliding inward as it should. I examined the mechanics of the front door for comparison, and realized that somehow the kitchen doorknob apparatus had been reversed. The curved side of the protruding latch was facing the wrong way.

I'm not particularly handy, but Marty is even less so. I got out the tool kit, removed all the screws and gizmos of the kitchen doorknob, and reassembled it the right way. It worked just fine from that moment until we sold the house three years later.

The following morning, a new poltergeist-y situation was upon us. I was working on my laptop in the master bedroom, as I did every morning. Each time I reached the end of a paragraph and hit the return key to begin a new one, the just-completed paragraph vanished into cyberspace! No amount of clicking "Undo Typing" would make it reappear. I tried saving each and every sentence, but nothing worked. It was as if some evil genie was determined to eviscerate my writing paragraph by paragraph.

This computer version of disappearing ink became old in a hurry. I gave up after half an hour. Later that day, when I caught up with Marty, I told him about my frustrating session. It turned out that during his own morning writing session, working at his own laptop in his den, he too watched his paragraphs get sucked into some microchip void.

After that single wracking morning, neither of us ever encountered that particular glitch again.

On the third morning after our Ouija-enabled conversation with Meta, I received yet another hint that some sort of negative energy was still hovering in our vicinity. It was around ten a.m. Son Charlie was in school and Marty had rambled into town to collect the mail. I decided to vacuum upstairs. When I opened the door to Marty's den, I noticed a poster-sized sheet of tissue-thin paper lying on the carpet in the middle of the room. As I drew closer, I saw it was a multicolor etching of an Indonesian demon: multiple arms and legs, bulgy eyeballs, and a protruding tongue in a leering face.

The drawing was technically dazzling, the content alarming. Not the sort of art Marty would collect—he was more into seascapes and Marilyn Monroe photographs—but I figured some pal had given it to him. I picked it up and placed it on his desk, topping it with a big, thick dictionary so it couldn't fly onto the floor again. Then I left to fetch the vacuum.

When I returned to the room, I saw that the demon poster had been shifted. Now it rested on the wooden seat of Marty's desk chair, with the heavy dictionary still on top.

Later, when both the Nadler boys were home, I showed them the etching. Neither of them had ever seen it before.

That was when I remembered the last stint with the Ouija board, and the spirit that had balked when we'd asked about God. I tucked the board into a dark green flannel pillowcase. Then I rolled up the devilish poster and stuffed it in a cardboard box in the basement along with the shrouded board. (Somehow I felt superstitious about actually chucking it; so flagrant a rejection might call down still more wrathful spirits.)

The poster promptly disappeared. That is to say, it never showed up again in future moves when I packed and unpacked all our boxes.

The Ouija board showed no inclination to disappear, however. In fact, it made me nervous enough that I was always aware of where I had stashed it. I knew it was in the cellar below my bookstore one spring day in 2007 when two teen girls visited the store in search of a Ouija board to buy. I warned them of the hazards and regaled them with the trials and tribulations with my own board.

They were still keen on acquiring one, as teens have been from time immemorial. I related the story of the girls in the summer house calling up Jack the Ripper. Their eyes widened, but they grew more eager than ever. I knew they would procure a board somewhere, come hell or high water, so to save them good money I gave them mine.

"If it gives you any trouble, just stash it in a cardboard box," I advised them.

I feel a twinge of guilt whenever I think of palming off that benighted board on those girls. But far be it from me to stop kids from monkeying with these sometimes diabolical tools. For myself, I'll never again place my fingers on one of those harmless looking Ouija planchettes. And if you try it yourself, intelligent reader, *caveat emptor*: never conjure up Jack the Ripper or Genghis Khan or even Casper the Friendly Ghost.

A Ph.D.
In Ghost
Hunting

Mostly what we look for in anyone telling a ghost story is a respectable résumé. The most creditable witness is a scientist, an engineer, or a math teacher: someone, in other words, who won't invent kooky stories. This way, when he or she relates the most bizarre tale you've ever heard, you quickly dismiss the thought that you're listening to the ravings of someone who has lost touch with reality. To the contrary, you assume the report is one hundred percent true. Has to be.

Such was the credibility of Dr. S. Ralph Harlow (1885–1972) who resided in Northampton, Massachusetts, and on the Vineyard at Lagoon Heights in Oak Bluffs. His anti-kook credentials were flawless: He earned an A.B. from Harvard, an M.A. from Columbia, and a doctorate degree from the Hartford Theological Seminary. An ordained Congregationalist minister, he was also, for more than thirty years, Professor of Religious and Biblical Literature at Smith College.

This was not your typical channeler complete with turban and crystal ball. Yet the distinguished doc frequently received messages from the back of beyond, and he wrote all about them in a book entitled *Life After Death*, published in 1961 by Doubleday.

In chapter three, Dr. Harlow describes a dramatic encounter with the ghost of his deceased sister, Anna, with whom he'd shared a lifelong interest in the supernatural. During their childhood, Ralph and Anna made a pact that whoever predeceased the other would send over the cosmic transom "clear-cut evidence" of life beyond the grave.

"Clear-cut evidence" was their mantra; there must be no doubt or mistake. It would be a grand science experiment with quantifiable data.

Sadly, Anna died in her early thirties, in 1925. Her bereaved brother was initially too distraught to even think about their sibling pledge. After the burial service in a Bristol cemetery, the professor returned to his office at Smith College to keep an appointment with a student.

They discussed William James's classic work on metaphysics, *Varieties of Religious Experience*. (Harlow writes with heart-stopping casualness, "[It was] a subject I had studied with James myself when I had been a student.")

In the way that we all fiddle with objects when we're turning over a thought, Dr. Harlow picked up a heavy glass inkwell that he used as a paperweight. He mused to his student, "Professor James once said to his class, 'How native a sense of God must be to certain minds.'" He set the inkwell down as his mind drifted back to the eulogies spoken at his sister's funeral. "Perhaps we can approach the varieties of religious experience if I tell you the religious experiences of my sister, Anna."

At the instant he uttered the name, a shot resounded, like a pistol going off right in the small room with them.

Both student and teacher stared in amazement at the source of the explosion: The glass inkwell had been cleaved thunderously, instantly, cleanly, and completely in half.

Then the disembodied voice of Harlow's sister said loudly and distinctly, "Is that clear-cut enough evidence?"

The student jumped up and fled in terror. She never requested another interview.

———

A short while later, Dr. Harlow's parents began receiving mysteriously charged messages. They would find them on Mrs. Harlow's bed table when they awoke in the morning. The notes were written in their daughter's hand, scrawled in blue ink on sheets of grey vellum. Oddly, the written lines ran at right angles to the printed guidelines on the paper. The writing did indeed look like Anna's longhand and showed examples of their late daughter's habit of stressing various words by underlining them.

The first note from Anna read, "I cannot find the words to express the joy and satisfaction of the work. We are busy every minute of the day, and sometimes into the night, too, but happy—oh so happy!—You must come and see for yourselves if you would be convinced. Do come all!"

Now there is an invitation! The fearless Dr. Harlow might have taken his sister up on the suggestion if the transition could have been comfortably managed. (Interestingly, while Mrs. Harlow found the notes persuasive, Mr. Harlow, an old-school Christian, declared them the work of the Devil. Disciples of fundamentalist religions regard anything to do with the spirit world as diabolical—no exceptions.)

———

On at least two occasions, Dr. Harlow intercepted messages from the Other Side while vacationing on the Vineyard. During a March weekend visit to their house on the Lagoon, Dr. and Mrs. Harlow learned that their neighbor and friend Helen had been diagnosed with cancer. Dr. Harlow later told a forum at Stevens Chapel (the Unitarian Church in Vineyard Haven), "[My neighbor] and I had many talks, including some on psychical experiences which seemed to comfort her."

In June when the Harlows returned to the island, Helen was alive and her immediate death "not expected." One day in July, the Harlows' ten-year-old daughter, Betty, went swimming a mile south on the beach. Suddenly she was overcome by a strong sense of Helen's presence. She dashed from the water and scuttled home. Bursting through the door, she asked her parents if their neighbor had died. Unbeknownst to the Harlows, Helen had indeed died at the same time that Betty was immersed in the water.

A few years later, the Harlows arrived for a May weekend. They celebrated their return to the island by taking a walk in the woods. "We especially loved the spring after a hard New England winter, for it is then that the fields and the woods are radiant with new life," Dr. Harlow later wrote in a religious publication called *Guideposts*. "The little path on which Marion and I walked that morning was spongy to our steps, and we held hands with the sheer delight of life. . . . This day we were especially happy and peaceful; we chatted sporadically, with great gaps of satisfying silence between our sentences."

They heard the murmur of voices behind them, and thought, quite naturally, that they were about to be overtaken by a group of people walking more briskly than they were.

Strangely, the voices were suddenly resonating, not only from behind, but from above.

"About ten feet above us, and slightly to our left, was a floating group of glorious creatures that glowed with spiritual beauty," Harlow recalled. "There were six of them, young, beautiful women dressed in flowing white garments and engaged in earnest conversation. If they were aware of our existence, they gave no indication of it. Their faces were perfectly clear to us, and one woman, slightly older than the rest, was especially beautiful. Her dark hair was pulled back in what today we would call a ponytail. She was intently talking to a younger spirit who looked up into her face.

"Neither Marion nor I could understand their words, although their voices were clearly heard."

The band of beings floated past them, their chatter fading until the figures disappeared. As soon as the couple could speak, they sat on a fallen tree, still holding hands, as they debriefed each other. They shared identical impressions, right down to the pony-tailed speaker and the rapt attention of her protégé.

It's interesting to note that the Harlows' already exalted mood, their sense of heightened pleasure at the beauty all around them, and their profound joy in each other's company, seemed to bring into their orbit this company of celestial beings.

This was a sight rarely conferred on anyone born since the time of the medieval mystics. The stirring vision must have boosted S. Ralph Harlow to a higher level of sanctity, although it's clear from his writings that he was three-quarters of the way there to begin with.

TISBURY'S
GHOSTLY
PERIMETER

hen an entire town is afflicted by the darker shadings of the spirit world, certain steps must be taken to shift the balance back toward the positive end of the spectrum.

The sweetness and shadows of downtown Tisbury (a.k.a Vineyard Haven) remind me of an experience Marty and I and some Vineyard friends had in the Uffizi Museum of Art in Florence, Italy. We referred to the requisite guidebook as we ambled from one brilliant painting to the next. In nearly every instance, the setting of each painting the book described as revealing—with subtlety, elegance, or even reluctance— "a veil of melancholy." Soon "a veil of melancholy" became our private joke for the duration of the trip.

But just such a dark veil is what the town of Tisbury has endured since the Great Fire of August 11, 1883.

—

The fire itself was a straightforward tragedy of the sort that was all too common in nineteenth-century towns. On that fateful evening, a fire started in the ugly four-story harness factory (located where the old stone bank sits today at the northern end of Vineyard Haven's commercial block). The old wooden structure, filled to the rafters with flammable materials, turned into a royal blaze in no time. An escalating northeasterly wind heaved the flames south and west. Before the night was over, the whole of Main Street and all the buildings within half a block of the factory had succumbed to the fire. Mercifully, no one was killed, though many were injured.

Much was made of the fact that no town fire brigade existed and that each shopkeeper and householder was left to his or her own devices, hauling buckets of water from individual wells and tossing them one by one on the fire. However, we might pause to reflect that a fire brigade in and of itself hardly guarantees full protection. In 1883, the Mansion House hotel, located at the far southern end of Main Street, burned to the ground without benefit of firefighters. The inn was rebuilt, but then in the winter of 2001, the Mansion House burned again down to its nub, even though the modern, fully loaded Tisbury Fire Department was located *directly across the street!*

Following the inferno of 1883, the township was so devastated that Boston and New York newspapers predicted Holmes Hole would never recover. They underestimated the pioneering spirit of islanders. The shops and dwellings of Main Street were rebuilt in the endearing style of a western frontier town. (It's inspiring to look at old pictures of this late-nineteenth-century remake because, while the shop names have changed, the buildings themselves are largely, recognizably, the same.)

So why did the veil of melancholy develop? Is it a psychical hangover from the horror of the fire? Certainly that's a factor. But, putting the pieces together, it's apparent to your average ghost-hunter that a negative vortex has opened up on the site of the old harness factory that was the incubator of the 1883 fire.

When I first began visiting the island in 1976, I thought, what a gentle history endows this place: no feuds, few murders, and only the smallest amount of chicanery. And that may be true: The Vineyard is indeed, and has always been, a kinder, gentler place than most of the rest of the country. But over the decades a reputation for extra sweetness and light has been generated, undeservedly, by reporters, editors, and historians, all of them unwilling to expose any kind of villainy.

Wouldn't you think that, in the aftermath of the Great Fire, at least one newspaper editorial or historical account would have posed the question of how the fire started?

I combed the *Gazette* archives, my own shelves, and library shelves for every last book, both archaic (locked under library key) and modern to see if anyone had *anything* to say about the cause of the fire. I found nothing. This was starting to feel like a thirteen-decade-old cover-up.

Such an untold story, particularly if it means a historical figure has never been brought to justice, can create a howling frustration in the spirit world (think of the Furies chasing ancient miscreants, or Banquo's ghost crashing Macbeth's banquet). In Vineyard Haven you can sense it on a cold November night when leaves clatter along past boarded-up captains' houses—or at Christmas as an oboe player brings temporary cheer to a street corner—or in the dead of winter during a long lull when no ferry steams into the gorgeous, empty port.

It wasn't until the spring 2004 issue of *Vineyard Style* magazine rolled off the presses that historian Chris Baer set the record straight about events leading up to that fiery evening in August of 1883.

This is the tale of a nineteenth-century Vineyard business-man named Rudolphus Crocker. Recently I asked a zillionth-generation islander and historian, "Do you know anything about Rudolphus Crocker and how he acquired orphans to work in his harness factory?"

The historian took a labored breath before he said. "Ah, my great-uncle Rudolphus."

Instantly I knew I wouldn't receive the real scoop on his venerated great uncle. Still, I persisted: "But was it true about his mistreatment of the orphans?"

He assumed the voice of a lecturing professor, "In Victorian times it was considered an act of philanthropy to provide lodgings and jobs for orphans."

———

Here's the unadorned, long-unreleased story.

In every age there are ugly buildings. Mostly we consider these eyesores a manifestation of the twentieth century, but the nineteenth century, cradle of the Industrial Age, has given us the worst offenders. In Vineyard Haven, one of those rose to a visually defiling four stories of grey walls and rows of prison-sized windows on the northeast side of Main Street: the harness factory and the dormitories for its workers.

Rudolphus Crocker was born and partially raised in Vineyard Haven, but at the age of eleven he was indentured to an abusive uncle who himself had owned a harness factory on the mainland. For five years he slaved away for ninety hours a week in his uncle's hell-hole. When Rudolphus returned to the island, he created his own hell-hole: a harness factory, first situated at the corner where Rainy Day stands today, then moved northward across the street, where the town's worst eyesore was erected.

Rudolphus Crocker's plant provided up to one hundred jobs and was the biggest employer on a jobs-scarce island. This alone must explain the pass he received from the local press. He was a prominent businessman; enough said.

His work crews were a rowdy bunch, mostly teen boys culled from the class of drifters, immigrants, and newcomers. When Crocker needed to beef up his work force he visited New Bedford orphanages, where he picked up eight boys at a time. The workdays were long and relentless. When workers misbehaved, Rudolphus whipped them. (Think of children exploited as slave labor in Third World countries today; this was the fate of America's impecunious kids in the Industrial Age.)

Often the boys would attempt to get free. On one occasion two of the lads grabbed a dory from the beach and rowed out to one of the dozens of tall-masted ships anchored in the harbor. Officials remanded them to the harness factory, where Rudolphus treated them to twenty lashes apiece.

News of Crocker's cruelty leaked out, and at one point the entrepreneur found himself under state investigation for overworking and horsewhipping his workers. No charges were ever filed.

The fire "of suspicious origins" (historian Chris Baer's words) started shortly thereafter.

——

Who knows what happens to sadistic bastards after they die? Although most of the more open-minded metaphysicians among us no longer believe in a literal Hell, we have a sense that those who've unleashed a tremendous amount of harm on others are, in the Afterlife, made to examine their misdeeds and endure a term of penance, perhaps by returning to human life and taking on the role of victim. In the process, these redeemed souls may help to shed light on the crimes for which they themselves were once responsible.

Fine. The karmic wheel is a wonderful thing, but back on Earth when a cruel man's memory goes down in old newspaper accounts and history books as a "prominent businessman" and the "Island's biggest source of jobs," well, that's where the veiled melancholy settles in until the truth is told.

Through the years people have confided to me about

ghosts apprehended in or around the old stone bank that stands on the site of the former harness factory. Robert Wheeler, president of the bank in the 1980s and 1990s, confirmed recently that the people who worked under him regularly reported paranormal occurrences.

"I never saw or heard anything myself, but I always thought the figure behind the haunting had to be old Stephen Carey Luce, first bank president in the early 1900s. He was highly germaphobic, so much so that he tied the guest chair in his office to the radiator to keep his visitors from getting close to him. He sounded disturbed enough to come back as an annoying ghost."

An excellent theory, but my money is still on old Rudolphus.

A woman who worked in the bank in the early '80s told me that in one of the corridors she often felt an invisible foot striking her ankle and tripping her. Most of the time she caught herself, but twice she took a spill that bruised her knees.

People have reported that, when walking past the old stone bank in the wee hours (on the Vineyard, the wee hours are any time after eight p.m.), they have heard watery voices coming from the vicinity of the building.

Long Island medium Inez Kirchenko, who accompanied me as my guest on my first-ever ghost walk in Vineyard Haven, intuited the following (before I told her or the group any part of the story): "I'm hearing the clattering of young men's footsteps. I see two boys running away from us up that dark street [where Main Street turns residential]. They're wearing heavy boots, frayed black pants held up by suspenders, long-sleeved white shirts, grey caps. Their hearts are racing. They're excited but fearful about getting away."

Diagonally across the street from the old stone bank, the owner of the French restaurant *Le Grenier* said that, back in the mid-1970s, he and his crew shared an odd experience as they reclined at a corner table, savoring cognac after closing time.

Suddenly a staticky noise swarmed at the street-side windows. A swirling white cloud formed in the center of the room like a slow-motion tornado. The owner-chef and his staff watched in amazement as the whirlwind swept across the long room, then percolated through a far window and disappeared.

A woman who as a child summered in a seaside home a few doors up from the bank, told me this story: "I was sixteen or seventeen, and backing my car out of the drive. Just before I reached the street, I heard the two back doors crunch open. I whipped my ahead around, but no one was there, and the doors were perfectly shut, as they should have been. Then after I reversed into the street, I heard the clunk of the back doors slamming shut! Again, no one was there, and the doors were undisturbed. It was creepy!"

There are ghost stories to be found all up and down Main Street. If you examine a map that shows the perimeter of the Great Fire, you'll find yourself studying the periphery of the chiaroscuro atmosphere of the town. It's a lovely village, and through the ages inhabitants have shoved back the darkness with flowers, charming shops, and human kindness. All we can do is bring on more oboe players, plant still more flowers, make an effort to smile more, and to open our hearts—continuously.

In a way, this town is a microcosm of all the human gathering places on the planet.

—

A postscript: In the summer of 2008, before this book went to press, another disaster struck Vineyard Haven when a popular eatery, the Moxie, burned to the ground on July 4. The adjoining building, which housed the legendary Bunch of Grapes Bookstore, was also scorched to the point of ruin. This is just the sort of calamity the town is prey to. At this juncture, the negative vortex appears to be widening.

Prayers are welcome.

MEMENTO MORI:
ISLAND
CEMETERIES

There is nothing more precious than a historic New England cemetery.

Whereas modern cemeteries are fully as banal as the suburban sprawl and strip malls that surround them, old burial grounds invite us to linger and reflect—the engraved messages on many of the aged tombstones exhort us to do just that. The visitor who heeds that advice comes away with a renewed sense of how fleeting life is and of how what lies beyond the grave is guaranteed to be better if we make every effort to be fully conscious in the here and now. In that regard, a stroll through an ancient cemetery is an act of meditation.

I used to wonder why tombstones of the seventeenth and eighteenth centuries were so grim. First you must come to grips with the death's heads abutted by angel's wings. (The wings are perceived by scholars as a sign of the soul's uplifting, but still . . .) In the Tower Hill graveyard, near the sea in Edgartown, Thomas Trapp, who died in 1719, rests beneath a slate that reads, "All You That Coms My Grave To See / Such As I Am So Must You Be." On Abel's Hill, in Chilmark, you'll see the 1747 marker for Elizabeth Bosworth, engraved with angels and devils in a pitched battle and the words *"Mors Certa, Incerta Die[s], Memento Mori, Fugit Hora"* (Death is certain, your days are uncertain, remember you will die, the hours flee.) And whenever the carvers were stumped for something new to inscribe that was suitably bleak, they could always fall back on the lines viewed in all old New England burial grounds, such as you'll find on Tower Hill at the grave of Henry Butler ("d. 1737 in his 37th year"): "When On This Stone You Cast an Eye, Remember You Are Born to Die." And there's always the perennially tasteful and pithy, *"Memento Mori."*

But the question arises, are cemeteries haunted? Well, yes and no, and some more than others. Ghost hunters Lorraine and Ed Warren, in their book *Graveyard* (St. Martin's Press, 1993), maintain that burial grounds become contaminated—and more susceptible to hauntings—when rude people bring in Ouija boards, black magic rites, and other demon-raising tools to rile up the otherwise neutral atmosphere.

This would explain the ultra-haunting of America's most haunted graveyard, St Louis Cemetery No. 1, in New Orleans. Of course, right away a cemetery is going to feel more haunted when no "inmate" is actually buried therein, but instead installed in an above-ground marble crypt, some of them as elaborate as mini-castles. You wander through these necropolises expecting at least one of the doors to bang open as the occupant lurches out, trailing decomposing strips of shroud. (The reason for these vaults is that the water table is so high, you could inter a body but it would float off in the next storm.) But the most likely reason for the countless spooky sights and sounds is that visitors are encouraged to bring their voodoo gear and to get busy with it, especially at the crypt of nineteenth-century voodoo priestess Marie Laveau, whose tomb is constantly layered with candles, powders, *gris-gris* bags, facsimiles of skulls—all that good stuff.

Here on the Vineyard we have no destination of this sort for voodoo practitioners, though we've always had our share of witches. Whether or not our beautiful old cemeteries—Abel's Hill, Tower Hill, and Causeway and Crossways in Tisbury—have ever been adulterated by black magic arts, the potential for spirit activity there is marginal, and here's why.

If we believe the anecdotal material of near-death experiences and the case studies of hypnotized patients telling of the spirit's state between reincarnations, such as those provided by Michael Newton, Ph.D, in *Journey of Souls* (Llewellyn, 2004), then we take it on faith that at the point of death we're pulled out of our bodies, able to gaze down at our own inert flesh and blood, then whisked through the stratosphere into areas of light and love and peace.

Now, imagine yourself in this great vat of wonderfulness. Would you ever care to go back to the place where your useless, cast-off body was buried? I don't think so!

You might return for your funeral, to send good wishes to your grieving loved ones, maybe even materializing in their dreams or as a loving entity at their bedside to provide them with hope and closure. But would you then take a detour to the cemetery? Nah.

If you were a tad overmaterialistic in your most recent life, part or even all of your psyche might take up residence in an earthly abode—perhaps in just one room of that house—*your* room! This accounts, I believe, for the lion's share of ghostly activity on this island that we've all adored—and continue to adore—perhaps a little more than was or is good for us.

But let's say the spiritually healthy soul finds the Afterlife infinitely more sweet than the human experience, which Zorba the Greek described as "the whole catastrophe." Would this soul come back at all, except to perform some helpful angel duties? Again, probably not. And would a helpful angel find humans to succor in a cemetery? The answer is, highly unlikely. When someone is prostrate with grief over a tombstone, the perceived wisdom is that the poor dear should be allowed to fully unload that particular quota of grief. Maybe the angel will hover overhead later while that person hangs laundry suspended on a line between two mulberry trees under a bright blue sky. *That's* when a jolt of life-goes-on-and-it's-darn-beautiful will be beneficial.

So what type of spirit life is left to frequent an old cemetery? The neurotics, perhaps, looking to see whether any family member ever slapped up a stone. (In island cemeteries, some slates appeared decades after the body *dis*appeared. Chalk that up to New England frugality and the high cost of monuments.) Then there are the above-mentioned materialists who are checking to see whose tombstones are bigger and more lovingly inscribed. Both sets of discarnate entities never received the lesson that our bodies are *not* us, that the moment we're sucked from our remains, our egos—our paltry, sometimes poisonous personalities—go *pop!* and vanish (except in the often burdened memories of our loved ones). If these sorts of ghosts ever waft into a cemetery, chances are they'll cut out the instant they realize there's little to mine there; they'll head back to their former houses where they can really, authentically annoy someone.

Also sometimes found creeping about these burial spaces are the baddies: poltergeists (i.e., beings that never were human) and ghosts of psychopaths who haven't yet been parsed by the blade of karma. Even without dark rites to summon them, they're bound to congregate where few positive buffers exist to keep them at bay. Hence your typical negative vortex.

During the day, ancient cemeteries are just what I described them to be at the beginning of this chapter: meditation retreats on life and death. At night, though, look out! As it's written on the Web sites of haunted cemeteries: *Visitors are advised that they go there at their own risk.* This is why I have mixed feelings about concluding my walking tours of haunted Vineyard Haven with a nighttime crawl through the elderly burial ground in the heart of town.

Cards on the table: I would never visit that cemetery alone at night. But with a group of twenty or thirty people? What a rush! Old tumbledown slates awash in moonlight? Absolute silence except for the distant hooting of an owl? Chalk-white hands that could reach out from under the ground, only they won't since you've got a crowd with you? I'm in! As I've said before, sometimes you've got to recognize that ghost hunting is just plain, goofy *fun*, and you go for it.

I've also got to admit that Long Island psychic Inez Kirchenko, whom I'd invited on my first Tisbury walk, showed her disapproval by remaining outside the gate of the white picket fence surrounding the cemetery. She told me later, in a manner that was nonjudgmental, only reserving the right to her own opinion: "I pick up so thick a blanket of mourning in a graveyard that I can't bear to expose myself to it."

I noticed that she also counted heads going in and coming out of the burial grounds, a hint that she also harbored deep misgivings about the harm that could be encountered there.

I do ask that my tour guests respect the grounds by observing perfect silence once we enter the gate. I have an abiding sense that chatter and any type of levity could create an atmosphere provocative to the bad boys of the occult world.

One tour night in early August, when we were about twenty steps into the cemetery, a little boy of about seven started to ask a question. I leaned down to his ear and whispered, "Can you hold that thought until we get back onto the sidewalk?" I continued leading the group to the heart of Crossways Cemetery, to the oldest slate, that of Abagail Daggett West, who died in 1770. As usual, I placed the lantern on the ground before Abagail's stone, and in respectful silence, all of us—as my groups had been doing all summer—brought attention to bear on this Colonial lady's final resting place, as my groups had been doing all summer.

When we returned to the sidewalk and I'd gathered the crowd for a farewell address at Captains' Houses Central (the corner of Church and William streets), I asked if the little boy who'd broached a question would care to speak up now. There were perhaps a dozen little kids on hand, and frankly, they all looked pretty much alike in the dark. "Which of you—? Anyone?"

Suddenly everyone in the group grew uncomfortable, especially me! People started to mutter to themselves words to the effect of, "Did a little boy ghost crop up in the graveyard?"

Finally a small child—a small, *live* child—shrugged off his shyness, cleared his throat, and piped up with his question, and a sigh of relief swept through the group, tour leader included.

———

On the premise that a little knowledge is not, as is commonly thought, a dangerous thing, but a way to impress your friends—provided the friends know less than you do—here's how you can show off your expertise in an antique New England graveyard.

The fearsome, but often fancifully rendered winged skulls were popular gravestone ornaments from the late 1600s through the 1700s. Of course you're not going to sound so scholarly if you give a slate that broad a timeline. Better to examine the amount of lichen on the base and the degree of erosion, and pinpoint a period (rub your chin while you're at it, and drawl, "Hmmm, I'm going to speculate post-Revolution by, oh, twenty years." (First step, of course, is to select a stone where the deceased's death date has eroded away, or everyone will know what a phony you are.)

The more cheerful carvings of winged cherubs became the icon *du jour* from the second half of the 1700s well into the 1800s. That's where you can call upon the subject's death date to preen even more. Because skulls and cherubs were both favored in the mid-eighteenth century, you can muse along the lines of, "It's refreshing to see a family opting for the more soothing graphic at this early date."

At the turn of the twentieth century, the sunburst—a rising and/or setting sun—came into favor, followed throughout much of the 1900s by the motif of urns (signifying mortal remains) and willows (representing mourning). No one did death better or more formally than the Victorians, with their black clothes, including widow's weeds, dark veils, even jewelry such as bars of onyx studded with diamonds, so while you and your friends stand before one of those urn-and-willow monuments, you might comment upon these funeral-happy ancestors of ours.

—

You're still advised to enter a graveyard in the nighttime at your own risk.

Someone who refused to take this advice is my colleague, paranormal investigator Bob Alger, whom I've mentioned before in these pages. Bob recently set up some equipment in the Burial Ground in the heart of Plymouth, Massachusetts; one of the oldest, if not *the* oldest non–Native American cemetery in America. As he moved through the dark, Bob felt a vibration run up through his leg as if someone below had taken a fist and smashed upward at his boot.

A few minutes later, one of Bob's cohorts cried out and grabbed his leg. "You too, huh?" Bob observed grimly.

In an e-mail to me, Bob once said, "On the whole, I believe cemeteries aren't particularly haunted."

Yeah, right. And nobody minds being punched in the foot from beneath the sod of a three-hundred-year-old grave site.

THE JAGGED EDGES
OF THE
SQUARE RIGGER

This was the story I didn't dare to write when I was compiling my first book on supernatural events, *Haunted Island*. I'll give it another go, and we'll see what develops. The worst that can happen is that I'll be forced a second time to abandon the project.

It was the late summer of 1993 and word had traveled along the local grapevine that I was looking for true tales of

Vineyard hauntings. A young Edgartown matron, Jane Tomassian, who sat on the board of the historical society, suggested I look into the strange doings at the Square Rigger. This restaurant at the crossroads leading into town has served drink and victuals for more than a hundred and fifty years. It's not difficult to picture the original tavern on a cold winter night, with a roaring fire in a wall-to-wall fieldstone fireplace; wagons, stagecoaches, and tethered horses lined up outside; wayfarers lounging around long trestle tables; pewter mugs steaming with hot rum and hard cider while, outside, wind-lashed oak branches tapped at thick-paned windows.

"The historical data is that the original family lived in the upstairs apartment." Jane said. Two brothers—thirteen-year-old twins—shared one of the bedrooms. One night, an electrical storm was brewing over Nantucket Sound. One of the twins stood at the open window, watching the storm move in. He was struck by lightning, and crumpled to the floor, dead. Legend has it that, ever since that gruesome night, the upstairs of the Square Rigger has been severely haunted."

That was all I needed to hear. I started making calls, the first to then-owner Will Holtham. He said that, sure enough, the apartment had seen its share of unearthly disturbances. He gave me the number of one of several members of that summer's serving staff who lived in the upstairs rooms. I tracked down the young man, who agreed that, definitely, a lot of weird stuff had been going on all summer: "Some of the other guys have woken up in the middle of the night because their beds were shaking. I myself, a couple of weeks ago, jerked awake with a feeling that all the air in my lungs had been sucked out of me. I had to sit up and take big, gasping gulps before I could breathe again."

I knew I was onto a good story and was eager to start writing up my notes. That evening in our seaside cottage, immediately following dinner, my son scrambled upstairs to finish his homework, my husband headed for his den, and I retired to my own tiny downstairs study to start my chapter on the Square Rigger.

———

I've always been skittish around machines, but so far I'd had no trouble with my four-year-old Macintosh computer (a techno pal had once described that type of Mac as the Chevy of computers: ugly, basic, but dependable). I was dimly aware of a distant rumble of thunder over the water as I started a new file with the simple heading, "Square Rigger." I began to type, setting the scene by describing the old tavern as the only light at the dark crossroads on the way into Edgartown.

All of a sudden my computer screen snapped to black and a strange, crackling, staticky white light gleamed horizontally across the center. I'd never seen anything like this before, and my reaction was utter panic. This is what a computer must look like when its hard-drive crashes, I thought. I pressed the control and power keys simultaneously to shut down the system. The white line sizzled and then vanished. The screen now faced me like a window pane looking out on a moonless night.

With a rush of relief, I recalled that, of course, we weren't supposed to use our computers when an electrical storm was brewing. (Back in the rustic days of 1993, that was the prevailing wisdom, anyway.) I reached down and unplugged the machine, and only a moment later the first zig of lightning flared around the house. Thunder rocked the foundation, and I darted off to make sure our two cats, Beebe and Gizmo, were safely indoors.

At dawn the next morning, feeling some trepidation that I might have shut down my Mac too late, I padded downstairs and powered up the computer. It blinked on perfectly, the system good to go.

For the next two weeks I labored on several writing assignments for a local paper, the aborted Square Rigger chapter all but forgotten. Finally, one sunny September afternoon I sat down to get cracking again on the electrocuted teenager and his—or someone's—continuing presence in his room. My fingers flew over the keyboard, a new, blank chapter opened up, and—the black screen with the crinkling, crackling white line was back! Once again I switched off the computer, but I didn't bother pulling the cord this time. I realized the sabotage of my poor old Mac had to do with the story itself, not the weather. And that's when I cashiered any further attempt to write about the Square Rigger.

But it's still a heck of a story, and I'm now working on a new laptop computer, so here we go again.

———

The Square Rigger evolved into the restaurant we know today in 1963. It was 1993 when my previous research unearthed stories of close encounters of the unpleasant kind. Some fifteen years later, the question remains: Is the upstairs apartment still plagued with unexplained—and unsettling—phenomena? The answer appears to be yes.

A few summers back I spoke with a waitress who was lodging in one of the upstairs bedrooms. She'd heard the accounts, of course, and that tends to heighten one's sensitivities, prod one's imagination, and turn the heaviest sleeper into a nerve-wracked insomniac. All of the above symptoms appeared to beset her.

One night she got to bed late—a little after two in the morning. She dozed off but awoke a short time later with an odd mechanical noise filling the room. It sounded like the back end of an industrial air conditioner such as you hear at a big hotel.

The young woman pushed herself into a sitting position, which brought her line of sight level with a double-hung window a few feet from the foot of her single bed.

"The drapes were open," she recounted, "I usually close them when I know I'll be sleeping late in the morning, but I guess I'd been too bushed when I finally got to bed."

Suddenly a man's face rose up from below the window sill as if slowly vaulted from a trampoline, then hovered outside the window. Framed by one of the lower panes, the face stared in at her.

"I can't say exactly what he looked like because I screamed, then threw my pillow over my head." (Little kids and ostriches hide their faces this way, thinking, if they can't see the scary thing, the scary thing can't see them. In rational moments we deride this maneuver, but it's precisely what even we grownups do when we suffer a freak-out of this order.)

The quick impression she caught of the face was of a grey complexion, raggedy dark hair sticking out in every direction, intense black eyes, but no mouth or nose.

As often happens when we're frightened to death, she pitched into a deep, escapist sleep—a little like fainting. When the young woman woke up in the morning, she decided she'd had a bad dream, but then her certainty was undermined by the sight of the open drapes; she rarely left them that way, and that *did* align with her memories of the night before.

There've been some other Square Rigger hauntings (of the upstairs; the restaurant is free of any supernatural reputation). The symptoms are fairly classic: sounds of whispering coming from empty rooms, cold spots, and sleepers disturbed by a shaking bed.

But now, in the early twenty-first century, this particular portal to the unknown may be gradually closing down, and one sign of that is that I have come to the end of this chapter with words and computer apparently intact.

SPIRITS
OF SINNERS
AND SAINTS

Is there a diabolical presence waiting to pounce outside the Federated Church in Edgartown? And can the counter-vailing benign forces inside the lovely old hall continue to keep the perimeter secure?

Good versus Evil is at the crux of every horror movie, and of the human condition as well. The battle is pronounced in the case of haunted churches.

I've never visited a church interior that felt maleficent in any way (and I've toured countless numbers of them, being the opposite of the traveler who says, "We've seen enough ancient cathedrals for ten trips—let's go get lunch.").

In the event that a church has attracted spirits, it's impossible for negativity to flourish (sorrow, maybe, or despair, but not for long) where all thoughts, all the time, are on God. To be sure, some churches over the ages have had their sanctity shattered by wrathful preachers. When Spanish and Italian priests used the pulpit to fire up the Inquisition, and English clerics damned Catholic heretics one year and Protestant heretics the next, those ancient cathedrals may not have imparted the very best of vibes. But milder periods prevailed, and, like a river protected from toxic dumping, a church can easily recover its healthy pH.

In Edgartown in the early nineteenth century, a church was built on South Summer Street, a block up from the harbor. Its lofty spire can still be seen from every part of town. From the start, the new house of worship was the focus of the age-old struggle between a controlling, spiteful preacher and a congregation keen to find the path to a merciful God and make their church a loving refuge.

Only one Vineyard historian, Henry Franklin Norton, wrote about Parson Thaxter's darker qualities (in *Martha's Vineyard History—Legends—Stories*, published in 1923 and still in print). Born in Hingham, Massachusetts, Thaxter graduated from Harvard in 1768 and rushed to Boston at the outbreak of the Revolutionary War. He served as chaplain in Colonel Prescott's regiment at the Battle of Bunker Hill, and that hero status anointed him for the rest of his life, stifling all criticism—or all *written* criticism—until Mr. Norton's book appeared.

Thaxter's Puritan meetinghouse in Edgartown was known as Parson Thaxter's Church because he had such tyrannical control of its members. Mr. Norton writes, "Parson

Thaxter was esteemed and reverenced but feared by the congregation." The historian provides anecdotes. Once, when the parson's serving girl broke a cup, he caned her. Another time he told a congregant who'd received prints of the gay life in Paris (*gay* in the original meaning), he hollered at her, "Hellish pictures, you old fool. Let us pray!" On another occasion when, astride his horse, he passed a parishioner lying sick beside the road, Thaxter sneered, "Trying to die, are you? Well, don't be frightened, for God don't want you, and the Devil won't have you." He ordered the man to get up and finish harvesting his grain field because the minister expected his cut of the ground meal. He even threatened the man with damnation if he didn't hand over the grain by sundown. The minister got his meal that night.

When at last Parson Thaxter's followers quietly revolted to follow the teachings of the Baptist and Methodist faiths, combining both disciplines in the newly erected Congregational (now the Federalist) Church, the parson felt betrayed for the rest of his life. The story has it that on random Sunday mornings the embittered preacher would stand on the sidelines and excoriate the worshippers filing into the chapel, doing what he did best: damning them all to Hell.

———

Who can say what caused the following apparition to appear—only once that we know of—nearly a century later in the brick courtyard outside the church? Was it a figure from the past? A mythological version of the larger-than-life Parson Thaxter? Or was it something wholly evil, sent from a place unconnected to this particular plot of consecrated ground? Perhaps someday we'll be able to pinpoint the supernatural as precisely as a GPS device can track an address three thousand miles away. For now we can only speculate.

In an evening in late November 1896, a woman born on the island but of Azorean descent, was finishing up her cleaning duties with a last dusting of the marble-topped table in the foyer. Fading light colonnaded in a golden shaft through the open door. The woman took a brass candlestick in her hand, wiped it with her cloth, set it down gently, then performed the same chore on its twin. When she turned to go, she noticed that the last of the daylight had died away outside.

From the top of the three-tiered stone steps, the woman faced a dark piazza of bricks. Next door, at the parish house, the windows were dark. She pulled the heavy mahogany door closed behind her. It connected with a soft thud and a click.

She turned, then froze in the doorway.

From beyond the expanse of bricks, an enormous black dog, the size of a calf, launched itself over a hedge, landing twenty feet away from her. He stared at her with eyes that glowed with red and yellow flickers like the core of a flame. No teeth were bared in the coal black face, but a rumbling growl emanated from its throat.

With just one more bound the beast could clear the distance between them and sink his fangs into her throat. The woman braced herself so hard against the door that she could feel the panels pressing against her spine. The dog lowered its head and crouched, then leaped toward her in a long, silent arc. And then it vanished midair.

The woman never told a soul in the congregation or in the town, but the story became her family's legend. She confided in her oldest daughter, who told her only daughter, who told all three of her children, one of whose daughters told me, at a Fourth of July party in the late seventies, at the home of my friend Nan Rheault, who lived on the eastern shore of the Lagoon.

Something about the story seemed to carry with it an oath of secrecy. All these years I've been waiting for another person to come forward with a corroborating sighting, but it seems to have been a one-time apparition—not at all unusual in the field of paranormal phenomena. As I've collected other stories of more gentle hauntings at the Federated Church, I've interpreted the element of the enormous black dog—the classic Hell hound—as a small but meaningful part of the picture. This is, of course, pure conjecture, but I have to think this unnatural canine has everything to do with the passions of Parson Thaxter.

In a kinder universe than the one to which that old Calvinist would assign us sinners, at least part of his psyche and soul may have been enveloped in the Light. But the other, uncontrollable part of him that dealt vengeance at every turn might have morphed into a beast to express his fury. Perhaps it is a beast that appears only once a century . . . if so, we're overdue for another occurrence.

———

One fairly recent story related to the church plays itself out like an occult video of a scene from the bad old Parson Thaxter days. A couple of years ago, as Vineyard psychic Sarah Nevin left a nighttime meeting of the parish committee and she stepped out onto the brick piazza, she heard the sound of a woman weeping in the narrow space between the church and the parish house. Moving closer, she came upon a heart-wrenching scene: a young woman, hunched down on her knees, face in her hands, appearing to sob as an older man lectured her. The woman wore a long, drab gown. The man was dressed in black with shiny buckles adorning his belt and boots.

Sarah had trouble distinguishing the words he spoke, but it was clear he was excoriating the girl, and she was duly humiliated. The drama, according to the psychic, was one of extreme cruelty. Unable to endure it any longer, she fled the scene.

———

As I mentioned before, the interior of the church contains an infinitely holier presence. "The sanctuary of the Federated Church is a portal to the spirit world," asserts Susan Klein, nationally known storyteller from Oak Bluffs. Here is her personal account (transcribed from a tape recording of her gorgeous, throaty voice):

It was the Christmas season of 1999, and we were recording a special Christmas CD at the Federated Church. Peter Boak was conducting the Community Chorus, and I was telling the stories. We needed the spacious acoustics of the church because we were doing a wonderful old version of "Silent Night." I was seated on the altar, behind Peter, staring at the faces of the choir for the next take.

So the choir sang "Stille Nacht" in the original German, and somebody's pronunciation was slightly off. After a couple of unsatisfactory takes, I was instructing them on the pronunciation when I was stunned to hear, all of a sudden, my mother's voice. She had a very distinctive, rich voice, and "Stille Nacht" had been her very favorite Christmas carol. (Sometimes, in fact, she used to play records of Christmas carols during July and August, blaring them out the windows on Wing Road for the tourists to hear, thinking they would enjoy this brand of entertainment.)

Well, there in the church, I followed the sound of her voice up to the balcony to the right of the altar. That's where I saw her. She was standing in a plaid shirtdress and a flowered apron, singing her heart out. It was amazing to me.

I knew I was the only one having the experience, so later when Charlie Esposito and I took the recordings back to his studio to decide which one to meld with my narration, we listened to all the takes and, sure enough, on the last one, my mother's voice was recorded. Charlie said, "This last one really sounds the best." and I said, "Yes it does!"

We used that last take for the CD. I gave

copies to my family members before it went out on the market. After playing it, my sister called me and said, "I don't think I can ever listen to the CD again." I asked her why not, and she said, "Because I can hear Ma singing."

Susan's mother, Ilse Henrietta Uienz Klein, born in 1911, had died two weeks before Christmas in 1995. Her voice can be heard on the *Silent Night* CD released by Ruby Window Productions, the title song recorded in the Federated Church in December 1999.

THE
LEPER GHOSTS
OF PENIKESE

A beautiful young ghost, once a leper, crawling into bed with you? Such an experience is not for the faint of heart. But this occurrence and many others, were taken in stride by Vineyarder Alex Friedman during his time at a high-risk job on the brooding and doomed island known as Penikese . . .

We might as well turn to Wampanoag legend to find out

how Penikese and its sibling islands off the northwest coast of
Martha's Vineyard were created:

> One day the Indians on Cape Cod called on
> their giant protector, Moshup, to help them out.
> They were being assaulted by Pukwudgees, little ten-
> inch-tall demons who made the Indians' lives miser-
> able by breaking their arrows, jabbing holes in their
> canoes, and scattering sharp objects on the hunting
> paths. Moshup gathered up a posse of his five sons
> and tracked the mean little critters through the wet-
> lands. But the malicious and clever 'wudgees crept
> up on the avengers, blinding and then killing the five
> young giants. Devastated, Moshop carried his dead
> boys to Buzzard's Bay, built up mounds of rocks and
> soil over them, and slunk away, his years of playing
> the Lone Ranger to humans abruptly ended. Mean-
> while the ocean rose, carrying the burial mounds
> way offshore, where they became what are now
> known as the Elizabeth Islands—Naushon, Pasque,
> Nashawena, Cuttyhunk, and Penikese

Of course scientists have advanced alternative theories
involving glaciers and something called the Laurentide Ice
Sheet and, later, the Wisconsin Glacial Stage to explain the
formation of the New England landscape we know today, but
the Moshup story sounds every bit as plausible, so let's go with
that one.

As early as 1003, Vikings may or may not have landed
on Penikese. In 1524, explorer Giovanni da Verrazzano may
have rowed ashore there; ditto French navigator Jehan Alfonce
in 1542, according to one published history of the Vineyard.
Definitely, English explorer Bartholomew Gosnold and a few
of his crew checked out the island in 1602, but he got Penikese
history off to a bad start when he frightened off four visiting
natives and swiped their canoe, leaving them stranded.

Clearly no one took the tiny, ladybug-shaped island seriously until 1873, when the Anderson School of Natural History was established there. This noble institution's sprawling and grand Victorian buildings—a laboratory, a dorm, a dining hall, and the Anderson mansion—resembled a mini Harvard overlooking the sea from Penikese's southern bluffs. Philanthropist John Anderson hired brilliant and internationally known scientist Alexander Agassiz to spearhead the new school. Unfortunately, Agassiz became deathly ill during his first summer on Penikese. He was shipped off island to recover, but died instead. The school lasted only one more year, and a sense of Penikese being jinxed has prevailed ever since.

So, where better to establish a leprosarium than on this sad and lonely little rock?

———

Humankind has had a shuddering dread of leprosy (now known as Hansen's Disease) for millennia, mainly because the disfiguring illness was incurable and untreatable. Nowadays it's still incurable, but it *can* be arrested with medications. It was also presumed to be contagious, but what folks never knew until modern medicine came along to educate them, was that ninety-five percent of people are naturally immune to it.

And, back in the day, its unfortunate victims looked phantasmagorically scary as their extremities were ravaged with lesions and eroded away by secondary infections.

In the United States, cases of leprosy began to show up during our great immigration waves of the late nineteenth and early twentieth centuries. The only prescribed measure was to banish these victims to remote outposts where they would spend the rest of their days removed forever from family, friends, the world. The rare affluent patient would be provided for in comfortable, albeit segregated retreats. The poor—most of them immigrants—were shipped off to facilities such as the newly inaugurated Penikese Island Hospital, opened in 1905.

The colony created controversy from start to finish.

Newspaper editorials railed against the proposed facility with rants such as this one in a Buzzard's Bay journal: "A national leper colony on Penikese Island will be a standing invitation for other states to dump their lepers. No laws can keep them out!"

Nonetheless, the plan moved forward. The old Anderson mansion was refurbished for head doctor Louis Edmunds and his staff, and small cottages were constructed to house the afflicted residents. Each building measured thirty-six feet by twenty-seven feet, with a kitchen, living room, bath, and two single bedrooms. The Massachusetts Board of Charity found five people who were willing to work on the island. At the outset, there were also only five patients.

Circumstances could not have been more miserable for those first inhabitants of the leper colony.

Frank Pina, thirty-eight, originally hailed from the Cape Verde Islands. After his diagnosis by Dr. Edmonds, Pina was removed to Penikese and his wife and eight children were forced to leave their rented cottage in Harwich and move to the far side of town. Town officials destroyed the cottage and reimbursed the owner with taxpayers' money.

John Roderick, thirty-four, a single man of Portuguese descent, arrived on Penikese, according to Dr. Edmunds, "Very sick, and slowly dying."

Isabelle Barros, another Cape Verde immigrant, was, for the first several years, the sole female patient. Back in her Wareham home, she had been nursed by her husband, but the couple had been obliged to give up their two children, a boy and girl, to become wards of the state. Isabelle arrived on Penikese, "Weak, anemic, and debilitated"—and, it turned out, four months pregnant.

Two Chinese men, Goon Lee Dip (twenty-three) and Yee Toy (twenty-five) were described as cheerful and courageous in spite of their obvious suffering.

In the beginning the frightened and lonely patients were skittish. They reacted to the sight of their caregivers by running away and hiding, refusing food, and generally behaving like feral children. In time, however, they grew close to one another and formed lifelong friendships. They grew flower gardens and worked on new buildings, and these outdoor activities gave them a sense of purpose, improved their spirits, and no doubt extended their lives.

Mrs. Barros gave birth to a healthy baby, though she was forced to give him up to become a ward of the state. Sometime thereafter, Dr. Edmunds pronounced the woman one hundred percent cured, but examiners for the Board of Charity arrived and refuted his diagnosis. In a fit of pique, the doctor resigned.

Dr. Frank Parker, with his wife, Marion, arrived to take his place. The kind-hearted couple would care for the sick on Penikese for the next fifteen years until the facility closed.

But, of course, the tiny island continued with its outsized woes for as long as the hospital operated there. Boatmen demanded higher fees to deliver supplies. Penikese workers were shunned by mainlanders during trips off-island. Voyagers sailing past would hold handkerchiefs to their noses, as if an aerosol leper germ could float to them on the breeze. Stateside parents threatened naughty children with stories of phantom lepers who would come to get them in the night.

In time, more patients arrived. As the illness took its toll, deceased patients were buried in a small cemetery over the hill (and, mercifully, out of sight of the cottages), bordered by a green picket fence and looking north to the sea. Most of the wooden markers have rotted away, although the Cuttyhunk Historical Society has made an effort to identify where the bodies are buried. Only four granite gravestones were ever put in place, and these have survived.

One of them marks the remains of Lucy Peterson. An immigrant from Russia employed as a maid in Brookline, the twenty-seven-year-old Lucy was shipped to Penikese two days after her early diagnosis. She was described as "pretty and well-formed" which was the condition her spirit assumed when it turned up in the bedroom of a young man some eight decades later.

———

The hospital closed in 1921 when all the patients were transferred to the new national Louisiana Leper Home in Carville, Louisiana (though not before outraged Carville residents launched their own NIMBY campaign against that new establishment).

From 1924 to 1973, Penikese was a bird sanctuary. The sanctuary's first warden, Mr. Turner, lived on the island with his wife and children until 1941, when a freak accident occurred. One of the Turner children killed a sibling with a hunting rifle. Shortly thereafter the grieving Turners moved away.

Penikese was unoccupied by human beings for thirty-two years. Then a new regime began, that of the Penikese Island School for delinquent boys.

Fresh air, plenty of outdoor labor, and the acquiring of good yeoman's skills—this was the protocol that, years before, Dr. Parker had instituted to provide a healthy daily regimen for his leprosy patients. The same good results were anticipated for the unruly boys of the Penikese Island School. However, of the original one hundred and six boys, tracked from 1973 to 1980, only sixteen turned their lives around. The others re-entered the world to wreak havoc, committing three hundred and nine violent crimes and more than three thousand nonviolent offenses in their subsequent careers. Once those results became known, funds dried up, although the Outward Bound–type school has struggled on to this day.

It was into this rustic morass of potentially dangerous youngsters that Vineyarder Alex Friedman stepped in the late 1990s to take up his new job as counselor.

"I worked on Penikese for six summers and five winters," he told me recently. "You work six straight days at a time, then take days off. You have to. It's a penal colony with ghosts."

Still, the idealistic and handsome young man (he's a lo-cal talk show host on Plum Television) expressed nothing but admiration for the Penikese school: "The boys and the staff built the saltbox house with their bare hands. There's no elec-tricity, so it's all heated with kerosene lamps. There are three woodstoves, one of them for cooking. Everyone works in the vegetable garden, chops wood, does repairs. If a window is broken, we're all motivated to fix it; otherwise we all freeze."

When new kids arrive on the island—they're called New Jacks—they're invariably skeptical and blustery about any talk of the supernatural. "Ain't no ghost, dawg!" is a typical response, Alex said, but the veteran kids tell them somberly, "You gotta respect the ghosts."

The Penikese boys, with nothing to do but work, study, and roam the eighty acres of the island, quickly learn every last detail of the history. Today's delinquents feel a common bond with the lepers, who suffered stigma and banishment even greater than theirs.

"They know the lepers' names and each one's personal history," said Alex. "There's an initiation ceremony for New Jacks. They're taken to the cemetery at night and they've got to do a rubbing of one of the grave markers. The staff allows it. It isn't a cruel hazing; it teaches the kids acceptance."

One night Alex, who loves to fish, packed up rods, buck-ets, and other assorted gear, and took a fourteen-year-old in-mate from New Bedford over to the north shore. "It was about ten o'clock at night when we walked back past the graveyard. This kid, Jimmy, behind me, started to yelp, in that indignant way little kids do: 'Cut it out! Cut it *out!*'"

Alex turned to see Jimmy slapping at his head, neck, and shoulders. "Something's touching me!" the boy shouted, clearly terrified.

"Come on. Let's keep walking," said Alex.

Jimmy continued his outbursts all the way back along the beach.

Sitting in my bookstore drinking herbal tea, Alex unconsciously lowered his voice as he told me the story of one of his fellow counselors, Kenny, a tough, karate-chopping ex–Army Ranger. "It was a summer night, and Kenny woke up to find a woman straddling him! Now, there were no females on the island, so it wasn't as if someone could have snuck over from a Girl Scout camp or something. He said it wasn't sexual. Her clothes were on. But she was reaching out and touching him as if she were hungry for affection. He said he kept thinking he was dreaming, so he tried and tried to shake himself awake until finally he had to accept that he *was* awake. Then, ironically, the strain of doing that caused him to fall back asleep. In the morning, when he told us about it, we all said the same thing, 'It was Lucy Peterson.' We'd seen pictures of her—she was young and pretty—and, of course, we were well acquainted with her gravestone up at the cemetery."

Alex's favorite of the Penikese ghost legends that have been passed down for the last thirty or forty years is one known as "The Man in the Yellow Pants." Here's how he tells the story:

Every year at Christmas, the school closes down for the winter. The kids leave, the counselors leave, and a local custodial staff—usually a single family—comes over to watch the house.

About twenty years ago, a mom from the Vineyard and her two kids, a little boy and a little girl, were the winter caretakers. One lazy afternoon all three of them fell asleep on couches in the big room. All of a sudden the daughter started screaming, 'Mommy! Mommy!' The mother and the son woke up to see a man standing over the little girl, reaching out to stroke her. His motions were gentle; it looked as if he were trying to soothe her and get her back to sleep. He had a long black pigtail, Asian features, and he wore yellow pants. Of course, anyone who's been on Penikese can identify him—Goon Lee Dip from the leper colony. Well, kindly as his ghost seemed to be, the family was terrified, and they left the island immediately.

Now here's the freakiest part. A couple of years ago, here at my house on the Vineyard, I was telling this story to a bunch of my buddies. One of them stayed really quiet the whole time I was speaking. Finally, after a long pause, when I'd started to wonder what was eating him, he said in a low voice, I was that little boy. I saw the man in the yellow pants. He was standing over my sister.

That witness, Eben Armor, had been unaware that the event from his childhood had become Penikese legend. Both he and Alex were astonished, too, at how the details of the story had remained unembellished over the years. Eben affirmed that, with a few minor changes, Alex's version— acquired third-hand or, more realistically, seventieth-hand —described exactly what had happened.

RANDOM GHOSTS III

No one knows the Vineyard's nighttime misty shores like our island fishing folk. These exploring men and women are particularly intrepid during the annual fishing derby that runs from mid-September to mid-October. If they cross paths with ghosts during their late-night bivouacs, they're disinclined to notice. A big green genie with shiitake mushrooms for ears could leap into sight in front of them and they wouldn't see it, not if the bluefish are running. Besides, these fishermen and women must appear as ghosts to each other, so many of them standing knee-deep in water, alone in hidden coves, gazing adamantly out to sea.

But my friend and ardent fisherman Ken Vanderlaske believes he may have encountered a ghost one cold October night during the derby of 1992.

"I had recently discovered Paul's Point [on the rugged northern coast of Makoniky in West Tisbury]. Not too many fishermen knew about it, because you have to drive miles down a godawful dirt road. And besides, those of us who hit on a good place, well, we keep it close to the vest.

"It was pretty late into the wee hours, and I'd been wandering along the pebbly shore, casting a line here and there, not coming up with much. I rounded a bluff and came upon a really secluded cove, but I was a little bummed to see someone else was already fishing it.

"He stood in waders about ten yards out. I could tell by his movements that he was a fly fisherman like me, so I started to think maybe he wouldn't mind if I took up a position—at a respectful distance, of course. Before I tried to hail him and get a little comradeship going, I turned to see where he'd plunked down his gear so I could stake out another spot for mine.

"Well, he had no gear. That startled me for a moment, until I considered how all of us sometimes get to meandering down the beach without paying too much attention to how far we've come from base. "That took about five seconds to figure out, and then I turned back to call out to the guy. He was gone. Disappeared.

"At first I thought—well, I thought a whole bunch of things: that he'd slid under the water, that I'd turned away for longer than I thought and he'd had enough time to move away. And, yeah, I thought maybe I'd seen a ghost. But I don't believe in ghosts, not really, so I dismissed the thought, although my overall feeling since then is, hell, yes, that fisherman was a ghost!

"I will say this. I ended up fishing the same spot, and not too much later I caught a bluefish that was the night's winner when I took it to the weigh-station. Maybe that's why I now think that guy was a ghost: Who else would fix up a fellow fisherman with such a nice haul?

"And, besides, I know that after I die, I'll tell whoever stands at the Pearly Gates, 'I'm gonna do some more fishing down on Earth before I can see straight enough to come back here."

———

People often wonder whether there are ghosts in Edgartown's grand old hotel, the Harbor View. Built in 1891 at the end of North Water Street, it offers commanding views of Nantucket Sound to the north and the Edgartown lighthouse and the bay across an open field. Well, of course there must be *some* supernatural activity from psychic imprints left by the tens of thousands of guests and staff over the decades. It's a well-known fact in the ghost-hunting world that, with the exception of hospitals, hotels collect a higher proportion of deaths per capita than any other square footage of property.

That's not surprising, when you think about it. Instead of the usual two- to four-bedroom single-family dwelling on that lot, you find a sixty- to one-hundred-bedroom behemoth. Right there, you're asking for more frequent visits from the Grim Reaper. And then there are the folks who have a need to check out from life itself, so they check in to a hotel so as not to discombobulate anyone in their home setting. On top of that there are the drinking binges that feel more appropriate and permissible while one is on vacation. These holidays with a bottle often lead to mishaps such as tossing a still-smoking match into a wastebasket or slipping in the shower. Weekend benders might trigger heart attacks—or blackouts combined with the nasty consequence of choking on one's own vomit.

The end result is a night watchman or a morning maid forced to confront a sad tableau. The authorities are called and, during a lull when few guests are likely to be in the corridor, a gurney topped by a black rubber bag is discreetly wheeled in and out.

Some of the most haunted sites in America are grand old hotels—the Parker House in Boston, the Coronado off the coast of San Diego, the Chateau Marmont in Los Angeles, where the Vineyard's own John Belushi (now buried in Chilmark) had his fatal overdose.

So . . . is the beautiful, Gilded Age hotel in Edgartown a repository of numerous ghosts?

Surprisingly, no. No one has ever come forward to tell me about classic hostelry disturbances such as smoke alarms going off at a stroke past midnight or thumps from a closet or a lady in white floating gauzily down the corridor, her slippers a good foot above the carpet.

Still, one thing did happen that I've filed under the heading of "Eye Opener."

In the spring of 1995 I was invited to speak about island ghosts during the Rotary Club monthly luncheon in the largest of the Harbor View Hotel's private dining rooms. During the Q & A portion of my talk, someone asked me, "Are there any ghosts here at the Harbor View."

"Nothing serious," I started to say, and at the same instant a *whomp!* sounded from the direction of the buffet table set up beside the tall windows facing the harbor.

We all turned to look. One of the flames beneath an open chafing dish had morphed into an orange ball of fire. Flames engulfed the silver sides of the dish, incinerating the food therein and extending fully four feet above in a mini-inferno. A server in a white smock rushed to throw the cover back on the dish with a clatter. Another attendant followed close behind with a fire extinguisher, but as he raised it to firing position, he—and his large audience—could see that the blaze had already consumed itself and was no more.

Ever since that time, when people ask me whether the

Harbor View Hotel is haunted, I take a deep breath and reply, "Maybe."

———

Canadians Doreen Kinsman and her husband bought their island home—the former rectory alongside Grace Episcopal Church in Vineyard Haven—the first day they went house hunting. "We were cranky and feeling rushed because we had to catch a plane that night, and this particular house was the only one we liked," Doreen explained.

The light was fading as they signed the purchase and sales agreement. Seated with the real estate agent at the table in the old-fashioned kitchen, they heard the sound of creaking hinges behind them. They turned to see the exterior kitchen door open by itself. No one stood on the doorstep. Shrugging, they redirected their attention to the document. The hinges protested once more as the door closed.

The Kinsmans' grown children, whenever they visited the old rectory by themselves, reported that the house was haunted. Unperturbed, Doreen agreed that it probably was, although, apart from the kitchen door incident, she had never seen anything occultly suggestive.

And then her friend, Margaret, died in Doreen's kitchen. Doreen herself found the body stretched out on the floor. Some ten years later, Doreen attended a Nathan Mayhew Seminar lecture by Constance Mesmer, one of the island's premier psychics. Ms. Mesmer made the rounds of the attendees and remarked on any stray scrap of information that happened to channel through her. When she stopped in front of Doreen, she cocked her head, amused, and said, "I'm seeing Winnie the Pooh and Piglet ambling along, and Winnie is saying, 'We'll always be friends!' Does that mean anything to you?"

Doreen shook her head. "No, not really." Constance shrugged, then went on to the next subject.

But later in the day a memory snapped into Doreen's head. Many years before, Margaret had sent her a birthday card with Winnie the Pooh and Piglet on the cover and, inside, a message: "We'll always be friends!"

The following year, Doreen attended another lecture by Ms. Mesmer, this time at the Katharine Cornell Theater on Spring Street in Vineyard Haven. Once more, when the medium approached Doreen, she received another dispatch from the sixth dimension: "I'm getting 'Thank you for holding my hand.'"

This time Doreen could pinpoint her late friend's meaning. Margaret had been nervous about flying, and whenever they'd flown together, Doreen would reach out to hold her companion's hand as the plane landed.

Only later did she realize another, deeper meaning: Doreen had taken Margaret's hand in both of hers when she found her friend dead on the kitchen floor.

———

In the spring and summer of 2003 I rented three-quarters of a house—the gathering room and kitchen area downstairs, and the two bedrooms and bath upstairs—from my friend, writer Jib Ellis. It was a Civil War–era house situated across the street from Eastville Beach in Oak Bluffs. The exterior clapboard was painted canary yellow below an adorable mansard rooftop with four dormered windows, two of them facing the sea.

Jib used the remaining two front parlors downstairs as his office. Although ostensibly he lived with his wife in her cottage on the Lagoon, from the time he prepared his first morning cup of coffee to the brink of six p.m., when he knocked off his daytime activities to roll home for dinner, he was in residence in the yellow house.

Along with Jib came his parrot, Felicity, who was given to the most godawful rain forest screeches, followed by the words "*SHUT UUUUUPPPP!*" which she'd picked up from a variety of humans responding in a uniform way to her own demented shrieks. This stretch of time marked a sad period in

154

my life. Charlie, my only child, had gone off to college, and former husband Marty and I had sold the last of our family domiciles to go our separate ways.

For the thirty years preceding my tenancy, Jib had rented to a series of bachelors, none of whom had ever taken it upon themselves to clean the place. Three decades of grime and detritus coated the rooms and filled the closets. A Brazilian woman named Glaucia, whom I'd hired to help me with the initial cleanup, spent a full hour and forty-five minutes on the upstairs bathtub alone. In the middle of her porcelain war, I found her on her knees in the tub, shaking her head and muttering "I don't know how people can live this way."

——

This background is given to explain my near-total retreat into the upstairs rooms. I whitewashed the walls and stenciled below the antique moldings for a royal-blue-and-white toile effect. I hung butterfly-wing-thin white linen curtains across the recessed dormer windows and brought in wing chairs and my four-poster bed. I could sense—whether I imagined it or not—a Civil War widow and several other females in her household embracing and blessing me for restoring tender loving care to this part of the cottage. Most of the day I was away at my bookstore in town, but on days off and through the long nights I hunkered in my upstairs hideaway, kept company by my cocker spaniel and my Siamese cat. And by the phantom females.

Jib had placed the house on the market, and by September the property had sold. Two sisters, Grace* and Tilda,* bought it for a summer home.

The sisters stopped by my bookstore to introduce themselves. They had the droll, dry accents of upper-echelon Yankees. Because they had plans for a gentle, much-needed renovation of the house—plans, in effect to take it from plain shabby to shabby chic—I thought for certain the Civil War widow and her female entourage would embrace the new residents as they had me.

Then one day I picked up a voicemail message from one of the sisters: "It's Tilda at the yellow house. Call me. Immediately."

Her flat and preemptory tone awakened my normally buried paranoia: Had I left a bag of trash in a closet, an inexplicable mess in the basement? It didn't even occur to me that, contractually, I of course bore no responsibility for the sisters' well-being.

When I returned Tilda's call, I discovered her interest in me was purely for ghost-busting purposes. Tilda had converted Jib's old downstairs office into a second master bedroom and Grace had taken over what I'd come to think of as the Civil War widow's dormered aerie upstairs. Tilda's bedroom, originally designed as a formal parlor, was surrounded by a shaded veranda.

Apparently for several nights running she'd awakened to a dismaying sight: "This has been happening every night at one o'clock in the morning. I open my eyes with a startle reflex. My bed is positioned so that I can see through both sets of windows to the porch on both sides. There are figures out there staring in at me!"

"What kind of figures?"

"Well, it's dark all along the front lawn, so they're kind of shadowy, but I can make out the shapes of a couple of stovepipe hats like Abraham Lincoln used to wear, and I can see some women in bonnets. Everyone seems to be wearing black. Or maybe navy blue or brown or dark grey."

"How many of them are there?"

"Some nights just two or three, other times a multitude!"

"Is there a porch light you can flick on?"

"Oh, I wouldn't do that!" she cried as if I'd suggested she run naked into the street. "That would surely make them angry!"

I reassured her that these spirits meant her no harm and told her to keep me updated, but I heard nothing further from either sister for more than a year. The next time I ran into Tilda, she told me the late-night visitations had ceased. She actually seemed disappointed.

It's funny how accustomed we become to our ghosts, and how much we miss them when they leave.

AN ATHEIST'S AFTERLIFE

y father believed in nothing. This Age of Enlightenment brand of "healthy" skepticism can be an obstacle to happiness in later years when the ailments of the elderly put a person in mind of what lies ahead. In the unbeliever's opinion, what lies ahead is nothing: blackness, emptiness, moldering in the grave.

Ever since I was a child, my dad and I debated each other about God and the Afterlife. (If he had written the preceding sentence, he would have left out the capital letters.) When I was young he would steamroll over me with his grownup rhetorical abilities and his contempt for what he considered the idiocy of belief in anything unseen. As I got older, though, and read many books, and my mysticism deepened, our talks became more mutually respectful.

"You're going to be pleasantly surprised," I sometimes told him regarding his fears of death and nothingness: "You'll find you're still here, there, or somewhere, and you'll be feeling mo' better!"

"I very much doubt that," he would say with the bleakest of sighs.

———

Dad's death was part of a ghost story in and of itself.

It was a hot and humid July week in 2000, and my parents, after a visit to us on the Vineyard, were house-sitting my Uncle Bob's 1960s-era split-level ranch house in Andover, Massachusetts. A year earlier, Bob's wife, Rita, had taken ill and almost immediately collapsed and died at the top of the staircase.

Mom and Dad found an eerie depression settling over them during their stay. My mom visited a superb medical intuitive in Newburyport, Joan Flynn, to whom she reported her sudden, inexplicable unhappiness.

With her hands on Mom's temples, Joan said, "There's a sad, angry spirit in the house where you're staying. She doesn't know what you're doing there. She's severely territorial. Are you sleeping in her former bedroom? I suggest you move to another room."

That evening my parents moved out of the master bedroom and made up a bed in one of the guest rooms. Sometime after one in the morning, my mother was awakened by an enormous *thunk*. She found my father unconscious at the bottom of the stairs. Had he fallen? Had he been pushed?

(Half a year later, Uncle Bob also took a tumble down these stairs, dislocated his hip, and spent months in physical therapy rehab. When he was finally released, he put the house with the cursed staircase on the market and moved lock, stock, and crutches to Florida.)

Dad lay in a coma for five days at Lawrence General Hospital north of Boston. My brother flew in from California and joined my mother, sister, and me at the vigil. On the morning of the fifth day, one of the nurses told us Dad's vital signs were flattening. He had only minutes to live.

I had a sudden impulse to call the Buddhist center on the island, where I'd been meditating and receiving the teachings. The lovely Lama Yeshe, a Buddhist *ani,* or nun, who'd been supervising the center, answered. I told her my father was dying and asked if there was a particular Tibetan prayer or chant that might be beneficial to him and to us.

Yeshe said, "*Om pani padme hum* is always suitable, but Sharma Rinpoche [the head of this particular Buddhist lineage] is visiting. Would you like to speak to him?"

Rinpoche came immediately to the phone. He asked me for my father's first name and then promised to retreat to the sanctuary and perform a *pow-wah* for my dad. (The *pow-wah* is a funerary chant to help a soul's transition to the *Bardo*—the Tibetan term for the posthumous spiritual realm.)

When I joined my family members beside my father's recumbent form, I marveled that, at this very moment, this dying atheist was receiving special attention from one of the major figures in the Buddhist world. At the same time that I entertained this notion, Dad's vitals began to recover, and he lived for another nine hours.

———

We decided to conduct a small memorial service for Dad at the Unitarian Church on Martha's Vineyard. Later that night, shortly after ten p.m., we stood in partial moonlight at the East Chop lighthouse and scattered my father's ashes over the *rosa rugosa*–lined cliffs. I quoted from Lord Byron:

So we'll go no more a-roving so late into the night
Though the heart be still as loving, and the moon be
still as bright . . .

The haunting started two nights later.

I had just dozed off to sleep, alone in my bed, when a man's voice—not whispered but at full normal speaking volume—crackled an inch from my left ear: "Time to get up!"

And get up I did! I jolted awake and pitched myself to a sitting position. It was the work of a moment to switch on the bed-table light. There was no one in the room with me. I checked the clock: It was a little after ten p.m.

On the second night, just past ten, my senses were sharpened and this time I was only half asleep when the man's voice barked again in my ear: "Time to get up!"

This time I flailed away from the sound, rolling onto my right side. As I lay there fully awake, the words still seeming to resonate in the room, I realized it was Dad's voice.

On the third night, again past ten, the instruction was repeated. By the fourth night my adrenaline level was elevated to the point where sleep was clearly out of the question. Pillows braced my back, and both my bed-table lamps glowed in the high-ceilinged room. I was alone in the house. Past ten o'clock, my glance strayed to the clock on the wall. Would my father tell me to wake up even when I wasn't sleeping?

At the moment I entertained this thought, I heard a footstep at the bottom of the stairs. Then another, then another. Someone was slowly, wearily climbing to the landing just outside my open bedroom doorway. When the footsteps seemed to place the visitor midway up the staircase, I called out dolefully, "I'm so sorry, Dad. I just can't handle this."

The sound ceased. I never encountered a trace of my father's spirit again, and later came to regret and feel guilt over my reflexive squeamishness. Why wouldn't I wish to hear or, perhaps eventually—if I'd let the sequence play out—*see* Dad's ghost? What could be the harm in that? In fact, wouldn't it be rather wonderful? In time dismay at that lost opportunity caused me to lose my jitters about the supernatural, which in turn opened me up to the phantom flurries of the past couple of years. But as much as I've tried to communicate with Dad, saying silently, "Come back! Come back! I'm not the sissy I used to be!" he hasn't graced me with another visit.

But others *have* crossed paths with him.

———

My old friend Laurie White, who, along with her husband, Peter, used to own the Old Stone Bakeries in Oak Bluffs and Edgartown, saw Dad on the evening of the memorial service. She looked up from her stove to behold a solid-looking, flesh-and-blood rendition of my father staring with palpable longing at the shrimp she was stirring in a copper pan. Before she could cry out, the hungry ghost disappeared.

When Mom returned to her condo in Palm Desert after a month spent grieving with her sister in Marin County, a neighbor knocked at her door. This man was a voice-over actor who also, as a result of a long-ago near-death experience, had a deep clairvoyant streak.

"I'm so sorry about Larry," he murmured.

"But how did you know? I just got home ten minutes ago, and I haven't spoken to any of our neighbors yet!"

The man nodded. "I just saw him at the mailboxes."

"But how—?"

"I saw what I call a transparency. He was leaping and dancing. He communicated great joy and pleasure at being here. He was so bubbly, he made me laugh. And he was laughing too!"

This, by the way, was right in keeping with my dad's personality. For all his curmudgeonly ways about life after death, he had the world's most infectious laughter.

Finally, my sister, Cindy, encountered Dad during a visit to the Vineyard in the summer of 2007. Let it enter the record that Cindy has never had a paranormal thought, insight, or tap on the shoulder in her life; she is truly Dad's clone in the skeptical department. Yet one evening as she dressed for dinner, she saw a gauzy figure of our father appear inside the closed curtains of the bedroom window. She took a step forward and felt a smile of incredulous welcome forming on her lips. He dissolved into thin air.

The following morning, with the apparition still uppermost in her mind, Cindy walked to the East Chop Light, where all of us gravitate to commune with Dad's spirit. She stood at the railing, gazing off to sea, speaking softly about the trying events of the past half-year, and how she wished she could feel his presence and have a stronger sense of him watching over her.

Behind her, bells began to chime. "It was beautiful, melodic. It reminded me of those old bell towers in Italy," she told me later when she returned to town. "I looked at my watch. It was seven minutes after ten. It seemed like an odd time for the bells to be ringing."

I said, "I'll tell you what's even odder: There are no bells at the East Chop Lighthouse."

"But I heard them!" she maintained.

"I'm sure you did," I replied with a grin.

I only wish I had heard them too.

THE HAUNTED PARSONAGE

The term *haunted parsonage* almost calls up the "Duh!" response for its redundancy, thanks to all those English mystery novels where every parsonage has an eccentric clergyman, a quaint history, and a ghost.

The parsonage on South Water Street in Edgartown, built in the 1840s, has all of the above. Back in the late 1600s, Governor Thomas Mayhew claimed this strip of waterfront property for his family. This land-grab was entirely legitimate, since in 1642 the man had purchased the whole island from a pair of English noblemen for the grand sum of forty pounds. (He also, on the same bill of sale, acquired Nantucket and the Elizabeth Islands, but liquidated these holdings when he realized one island was sufficient for his needs.)

The Mayhews were political animals, but they also bred religious zeal in their gene pool. Thomas Mayhew, Sr., and especially Thomas Mayhew, Jr., made it their mission to convert the Indians. This responsibility to church and faith extended down through the lineage to Sarah, the last of the Mayhews to own the Water Street property. When she died in 1956, she bequeathed her house to the Federated Church on South Summer Street (also haunted—see chapter 17) as the lodging for its minister.

The current pastor, the Reverend Gerry Fritz, says he's constantly approached by Mayhew descendants from many separate branches of the Colonial-era family tree, who contend, "You're living in my house!" The Reverend Fritz says he's lucky he knows the straight line of descent that preceded Sarah's bequest, or he might be concerned about having to run a hostel for nomadic Mayhews.

I had heard stories over the years about the spirit life at the parsonage. A single phone call answered my question.

"Is the parsonage haunted?" I asked the voicemail for the Reverend Fritz.

He called back the next day. "Indeed it is."

Two mornings later I sat in the clergyman's cozy, book-laden office in the parish hall beside the church. What followed was one of the most fascinating interviews I've ever conducted.

———

Gerry, his wife, Kathleen, and their daughter, Katelyn, moved into the parsonage on October 11, 1999. After putting Katelyn to bed, the couple gravitated to what they called the Blue Room downstairs, a small, inviting study facing the harbor. The night was chilly, so the windows were closed. Gerry sat on one end of the sofa, and Kathleen stretched out with her head on his lap. On the far side of the room sat a television bracketed by two old rocking chairs.

Not long after they'd settled into the cushions, one of the chairs began to move back and forth. This was more than just a quiver; it was a good, solid rocking movement, as if a hundred-plus-pound person were sitting there. The rocker moved back and forth for ten or fifteen seconds, then stood as still as the other chair.

Kathleen rose from her horizontal position. Husband and wife stared at one another, then Kathleen said, "Must be Sarah." She turned to face the chair and voiced the absolutely correct protocol of living inhabitant to dead proprietor: "Hello. We'll be living here for awhile. We love this house and we promise to take good care of it."

From time to time over the following years, "Sarah" continued rocking in her favorite chair beside the television.

Another form of haunting was olfactory: Gerry would often walk into a room and encounter an overwhelming fragrance of flowers. "There would be no bouquet in the room, no windows open onto the garden. It was always a scent arising from nowhere, but an absolutely wonderful surprise."

One afternoon, Kathleen came downstairs and saw the figure of a woman standing in one of the doorways. The woman wore a tailored, dark, Depression-era skirt and jacket. "Hello, Sarah," she said, and the apparition vanished.

Once, during the Christmas season, Gerry delivered a sermon with a title borrowed from the hymn "In the Bleak Mid-Winter." Afterward, he strolled home in weather that seemed to take its cue from the song. Arriving back at the parsonage, he glanced at an upstairs window where a light glowed; a talisman against the grey skies. A woman stood framed in the window. Gerry assumed it was Kathleen, and he gave her a merry wave.

Several seconds later he bumped open the back door and crossed the threshold of the kitchen to find his wife standing at the stove with her back to him.

"What are you doing here?" he asked in surprise.

She turned her head and cocked him a look. "Ah . . . I live here."

"But I just saw you upstairs at the bathroom window!"

"I haven't been upstairs in over an hour."

Gerry trudged to the second floor and inspected all the rooms. No one else occupied the house. Unless they counted Sarah, which, in fact, they did.

"Sarah likes me!" Gerry said. "That's the feeling I get. She liked men, apparently, but not necessarily in a flirtatious way. She simply enjoyed male company. A few days after her appearance at the window, it was Christmas Day, and the three of us were opening our presents. At the bottom of my Christmas stocking I found an old, tattered antique handkerchief. There was a little bit of embroidery on it, and the initials S.M. "Where'd you get this?' I asked Kathleen. She replied, 'I've never seen it before.'"

A final, comical ghost occurrence: The Fritzes' fat, stubby-legged terrier/dachsund mix, Pepper, always slept with Gerry and Kathleen, but was physically incapable of climbing up on their extra-high bed without help. On nights when husband or wife left the bed, Pepper often would insist on being removed from the mattress and placed on the floor. But then, when the wandering spouse returned, Pepper would be back on the bed, with the recumbent spouse still sound asleep.

The Fritzes' acceptance of the ghost at the parsonage led to an interesting follow-up involving a local myth; the kind we all deride as fodder for kids' tales at pajama parties.

Virtually every country locale has its version of the Abandoned Bride yarn, which invariably involves the following plot points: Bride is jilted by groom, bride gets killed or kills herself at some spooky spot in the countryside, bride clad in white wedding gown returns on moonless nights to the scene of her death, where the hapless sojourner is bound to encounter her.

Shortly after the Fritzes moved to Edgartown and became acquainted with the ghost of Sarah Mayhew, they took a road trip back to their former town of Machias, way down east on the coast of Maine.

"If you get off the main highway, there's a more direct alternate route that winds through heavy woods around a remote lake," Gerry told me. "It's called Catherine's Hill, and the story goes that Catherine was traveling this road on her way to her wedding, dressed in her white gown, alone in a horse-drawn buggy. Some accident befell her, the buggy overturned, and she was killed. Of course, legend has it that people driving around this lake late at night have seen this ghost bride."

It was around eleven at night when Gerry and Kathleen, with Katelyn asleep on the back seat, reached Catherine's Hill. Gerry joked to his wife, "You know, now that we're on good terms with Sarah at the parsonage, maybe it'll open up a portal for us to see poor Catherine."

At that moment, the headlights of the car picked up something glowing ahead of them at the side of the road. As they drew closer, they discerned a young woman in a trailing, lacy white gown. Her back was to them, and she walked determinedly as if there were no automobile chugging behind her.

The Fritzes stared in shock as they approached. An actual, living person stranded—for whatever reason—on this pitch black road, would turn to flag down a passing vehicle, but this woman ignored them (or was oblivious to them), and never broke stride.

As they drew abreast of her, they had an impression of a pale face, a cloud of gold hair, and a long, bedraggled white dress.

"Should I stop for her?" whispered the good-hearted clergyman, removing his foot from the accelerator to hover over the brake.

"*No!*" cried Kathleen.

The panic in her voice made Gerry step on the gas. They kept on driving and the sight of the lost bride vanished from their rearview window as they rounded the next bend.

—

Gerry Fritz is a sprightly, fifty-something man with a head of bushy silver curls shorn short. He's the dream minister in that you feel you can tell him anything. So I did, once I'd finished jotting my notes from our interview.

A memory had been slow-cooking in my consciousness for several days, and I had been waiting for the perfect person to share it with. I prefaced it by explaining my belief that emanations from the spirit world are just the starting point for our seeking, that there exist supernatural happenings of another, higher order that connect us with the Divine.

"Something happened to me some forty-three years ago," I continued. "All this time I've been waiting for the proverbial scientific explanation, expecting to come across a description of the same phenomenon in a *National Geographic* article, or hear a similar story from another person, but that hasn't happened. And in light of all the odd and wonderful experiences I've had, I've come to the conclusion that science had nothing to do with it. All those years ago, several high school friends and I were gifted with a miracle."

I had his attention. His dark grey eyes stayed fixed on my face as he nodded for me to go on.

It was a July night in 1965. My friends and I had staked out a secluded cove of Zuma Beach on the Malibu coast. We'd built a campfire. I'm sure some beer was consumed, though I've never been a beer drinker myself. I sat alone for a while on the outskirts of the group, and at a certain point an unusual mood settled over me. At the time I had no frame of reference for it, although many years later I realized it was a state of Grace. Certainly during my young life I'd known pleasure and comfort and excitement. But this was altogether different. Even at the time I knew it was somehow bound up in holiness, even though my upbringing (Judaic heritage, Unitarian Sunday school) had given me no vocabulary for this brand of divinely inspired transformative state.

Then someone suggested we go for a walk.

The minute our bare feet touched the wet sand of the high-tide line, geysers of shiny sparks erupted from each footstep, splashing up into the air. This wasn't a mere brief flare of phosphorescence—these were clouds of sparkles gusting all around us as if a sugar plum fairy with hands the size of catcher's mitts reached into a sack and tossed out showers of glitter.

We not only walked along the beach, we strutted and hopped and performed jumping jacks, and those of us who'd taken ballet classes did *fouette* turns and *tours jeter*. We gamboled for at least an hour—maybe two, maybe three. My memory stops at the point when we at last turned our backs on the beach, packed up, and went home.

All that remains is a sense of transcendent beauty and a gift of holiness that I've been waiting all my life to recover.

—

The Reverend Fritz reflected for a moment. Then softly he told me of his own first experience with the Sacred.

In another life, as he called it, Gerry was a banker with a wife and two kids (since divorced and grown, respectively). He'd formed a friendship with a man who was studying to be a minister, and this friend informed Gerry that he, too, would be called to the cloth.

"Not a chance!" responded Gerry with a hoot of laughter. "I like my way of life, especially the security and this little thing called money."

When his friend's time came to be ordained, he invited Gerry to attend the ceremony and gave him a special assignment. Thirty appointed friends and colleagues would be placing their hands, pancake style, on top of the new minister's head. "I want yours to be the first hand," he told Gerry.

When the moment arrived, Gerry applied his hand gently ("If you press too hard, the weight of the other hands will drive me to the floor," his friend had warned). As the thirtieth hand came to rest above all the others, Gerry felt an enormous wind blow through the cathedral.

"It surged through and roared in my ears and swirled around me as if I might levitate. When it finally faded away and we all removed our hands, I asked the man nearest me, 'Does that always happen?'"

The man regarded him blankly. "Does what always happen?"

"The wind!"

A continuing blank stare.

Gerry asked some of the other participants as well, but no one seemed to know what he was talking about. Finally he faced his friend, the newly ordained minister. "Did *you* feel it?"

His friend's face glowed from within. "Didn't I tell you?"

A short time later, Gerry began planning his return to college in preparation for entering the seminary.

——

Our local National Public Radio station airs a regular show by a Vineyard bird-watcher named Vernon Laux. He always signs off with, "Keep your eyes to the sky!"

I'd like to make the same recommendation, but not for the purposes of bird-watching, although that's certainly a worthy activity. I can't emphasize enough how rewarding it is to keep our eyes to the sky, to the sea, to the fields, to the faces of all the people who pass us on the street. Each one of us is given opportunities to behold awesome—in the fine old sense of the word—sights and sounds. And sometimes these sights and sounds have an origin that we regard as supernatural.

I believe that whether it's a bird on the wing or departed Aunt Cecily rapping on our walls or a sudden sense of oneness with all Creation, all these gifts are sent to us by the same Source.

ACKNOWLEDGMENTS

My profoundest thanks go to my editor, Karin Womer, at Down East Books—this is our fourth book together, so between us we've demolished a whole acre of forest. Many thanks to intrepid archivist Eulalie Regan at the *Vineyard Gazette,* who played the Watson to my Holmes (or maybe the other way around) when she learned no one had ever written truthfully about Rudolphus Crocker and his part in the Great Fire of 1883. Also Eulalie has placed in my hands countless envelopes with clippings about fascinating islanders whose lives have intersected with so many of these stories. And, speaking of old Rudolphus, thanks are in order to Charlie Utz, publisher of *Vineyard Style Magazine,* and historian Chris Baer for being the first to break the real story.

And speaking of the *Vineyard Gazette,* many thanks to editor-in-chief Julia Wells, editors Lauren Martin and Jim Kinsella, and everyone else in that venerable newsroom, who extends a warm welcome whenever I visit. I also love it that they let me write about everything under the sun, including ghosts, in my weekly town column.

I appreciate all the help I've received from the folks at the Oak Bluffs Library: Danguole Budris, Matthew Bose, Anita Parker, Pamela Speir, and Rosemary Hildreth.

I'm grateful to Vineyard Haven psychic Karen Coffey for sending me down some most intriguing paths. Robert Alger, of Pilgrim Paranormal Research, has been an invaluable resource and generously allowed me to use one of his photographs in the book. It's been fun hanging out with him and his cohorts, Patrick McAllister and Bob Kent, on ghost-hunting stakeouts, and a huge extra thanks to Pilgrim Paranormalists Scott Stalter and Donnie Reese for building my Web site, www.Vineyard Ghosts.com.

Over the years, thousands of people have participated in my ghost walking tours, and the accounts many of them have imparted during the hour we spend together have contributed to my own personal Wikipedia of the supernatural. Thanks also must go out to all the island spirits who've found a way to make me sit up and take notice—life is so much more magical when they're out and about.

Thank you, too, to my fantastically loving, talented, supportive, and hilarious son, Charlie, now living in Los Angeles and following the promptings of family genes to be a writer. To my sister, Cindy; mom, Trina; brother, Owen; and sister-in-law, Faith: thank you for being in my life. Much love and gratitude to Marty Nadler, the best ex-husband in the world. My pets, Huxley and Beebe, are hardly the best dog and cat in the world, but they keep me laughing. My heart always warms to my closest women friends on the Vineyard; in alphabetical order, Donna Bubash, Paula Catanese, Jessica Harris, Injy Lew, Gwyn MacAllister, Lisa Rohn, Marcia Smilack, and C.K. Wolfson.